Hoofmarks

Hope Sawyer Buyukmihci

J.N. Townsend Publishing
Exeter, New Hampshire
1994

Printed in the United States by BookCrafters.

Published by

J. N. Townsend Publishing
12 Greenleaf Drive
Exeter, New Hampshire 03833
(603) 778-9883

First Printing.

Catalogue-in-Publication Data
Buyukmihci, Hope Sawyer.
Hoofmarks / Hope Sawyer Buyukmihci
p. xm.
1. Human-animal relationships--New York (State)--Nonfiction. 2. Domestic animals--New York (State)--Nonfiction. 3. Farm life--New York (state)--Nonfiction. 4. Pastoral nonfiction, American. I. Title.
PS3552.U895H66 1994
813'.54--DC20 94-10664
CIP

Other Books by Hope Sawyer Buyukmihci

Hour of the Beaver
Beaversprite
Unexpected Treasure

Contents

Two to Grow

GRANDPA'S chestnut gelding Prince was the first horse I ever drove. The summer I was four, Grandpa and I drove Prince each morning to the milk factory. Before the Plymouth Rock rooster crowed twice I was out of bed. I slid my gingham dress over my head. The screen door banged as my bare feet scurried through the grass to the barn, where Grandpa had swung the east door open so the cows could come in for milking. The work horses, Baron and Big Tom, munched grain in their stalls. Beyond them stood Prince, already harnessed.

Grandpa stood at the door. He was a lean dark man, not tall, with a heavy, sweeping mustache. His faded blue eyes behind steel-rimmed glasses matched his worn overalls. Old Blue, the bell cow, came in first, a crochety dame with one crooked, sawed-off horn, her hairy white sides freckled grayish blue. As she waddled over the high step, the square Swiss bell on her collar clanged. She passed to her stall, stepped over the gutter and thrust her head through the open stanchion. Grandpa called to the other cows, "Get in here, Bess. Maltie, quit shoving. We haven't got all day."

His voice was stern. When the cows were in, he limped down the row of stanchions on his crippled leg that had not been set right after the team ran away and the wagon wheeled over him. He locked each stanchion firmly against a slender neck. "Now we'll make the pies." He scooped feathery bran into a pail, and from a barrel he dipped a pailful of blackstrap molasses. Hobbling down the aisle in front of the cows, he put a scoop of bran and a dipper of molasses in each manger. "Cows like their pie just like me and you," he said. Wood creaked and chains rattled as the cows strained against their stanchions to reach the last drop. At the barrel I dunked a finger and licked it. Ugh, the molasses was bitter.

Grandpa took a pail and swung the milk stool from its peg. "So-o-o, girl, so." He plunked down beside the red heifer, Sal. "Bring your cup," he told me.

I dashed to the spring house and stood on tiptoe to reach the tin cup that hung on a nail. It was dusky and chill in the spring house. The battered cup felt cold in my hands as I leaned over the spring, where pollywogs darted—black dots above the sand. The water bubbled from one corner, flowed under the milk-cooler, then out clear and fresh to make a brook in the barnyard. From there it wound through the pasture to join the river.

Grandpa took my cup in one hand and a flexible pink teat in the other. With a few squeezes he filled the cup till it foamed over. I drank it down, warm and delicious.

"More?" asked Grandpa.

"No, thank you." At the spring, I rinsed my cup and

stretched to hang it back. Then I sat on the cement curb and let my feet dabble so the pollywogs could nibble my toes.

Grandpa brought pail after pail of milk. Through a strainer he poured it into tall cans set into the cooler frame. Water reached half way up their sides. As the cows filed past on their way to pasture Grandpa took the metal plunger and began to cool the milk. The funnel fitted into the necks of the cans and Grandpa worked the handle up and down. He counted under his breath, so many strokes to a can. The water flowed around the cans to impart coolness.

Prince was hitched to the milk wagon. The cans were in place. Grandpa mounted the seat and reached to pull me up. From the high seat I craned my neck to watch the wheels lift dry rivulets of sand as they turned down the driveway. Before us stretched River Road, level all the way into town. It curved with the river and as Prince spanked along we passed under arches of willows where birds sang.

For a while I watched the dusty grass flash by and listened to the birds. Grandpa drove with the lines threaded between thumb and fingers, one hand on his knee, the other at rest. "Want to drive?" he asked, and handed me the lines. I clutched one in each hand.

"Easy," he said. "Don't hold the lines too tight." As Prince tossed his head the lines kept loosening and Grandpa had to help me fix them back.

At the factory, men dumped our milk into a big vat and we drove home. Grandpa took Prince's harness off and turned him out to pasture, where the first thing he did was get down and roll. Legs in air, he threw his weight to tip his body to the other side. He tried several times, waving his legs and grunting. At last he made it, rubbed his other side in the dirt and rose with a bound. He shook himself and began to graze.

"May I curry Prince, Grandpa?"

"No, he's a biter and a kicker. Don't go near him when he's not in harness."

I ran to the house ahead of Grandpa, and found Grandma at the kitchen stove frying pancakes, a flowered apron over her blue-sprigged dress.

"Hurry and wash up," she said. "Breakfast's ready." Her smile was framed by her soft white hair. She gathered pancakes from the griddle, added them to the stack in the warming oven and poured more batter.

I washed my face at the sink and ran to the table. From there I watched Grandpa, who pumped the basin full, laid his glasses on the shelf, and plunged his face in. He came up dripping and fumbled blindly for a towel. At the head of the table he sat in a straight armchair—a captain's chair—and stretched his stiff leg out to one side. "Dish up, Lib," he said. "It's late and I want to get that corn planted today." Grandpa bowed his head. "Dear Father, we thank Thee for this food. Help us to do Thy will today. Amen." I kept my head bowed, but I peeked at the food.

Grandma heaped my plate with crisp brown-fried potatoes, golden pancakes and fluffy eggs. I poured milk into my Postum until the cup was full. On my pancakes I spread butter and poured on rich maple syrup.

When Grandpa'd had enough he wiped his mustache. "Good vittles, Lib," he said. As he got up he asked, "Who's going to help me plant corn?"

"I am." I jumped down and raced to beat him out the door.

In the barn he took the planter from its high dusty hook. "Bring a rag," he commanded. "And some oil."

Grandma gave me a faded blue shirt and brought the oil can from the cellarway. "Dar never knows where anything is," she muttered. "He ought to keep these things in the barn." I bunched the clean shirt under my chin.

As I held the can of oil Grandpa wiped away cobwebs from the planting machine. He rubbed disc and cog and laid them in orderly fashion on the bench beside him. He squinted inside the cylinder, blew out reluctant spiders and wiped the inside clean. He eased himself from the bench with a grunt. "Go get the corn," he said. "Your grandma knows where it is."

"Land sakes, is that in here too?" she scolded. She found it on a shelf in the woodshed. "That man'd lose his eyes if they wa'n't fastened in." She settled the heavy bag in my arms. "Now shoo, and let me get to my work."

It wasn't far to the corn field. Grandpa carried the planter and the sack, and I carried the hoes. We set our loads down at the edge of the plowed field. The day before I'd driven Prince on the marker so Grandpa could mark the field in squares. Beyond the field was a line of maples. From one branch still hung the red rag to which Grandpa had sighted when he set the plow for the first furrow. A robin sang in an apple tree at the corner and blackbirds were busy in the harrowed dirt. A killdeer landed. He weaved among the clods, his tan plumage set off by twin collars of black. The sun looked like a giant orange.

"Sky red in the morning, sailor take warning," quoted Grandpa. "It'll rain before night." He undid the sack and I burrowed my hand deep among the kernels. "Don't play," he said. He held the planter upright between his knees and reached for the sack. As pale gold kernels poured out, dust spirals rose in the sunny air.

"Let's go," he said and stepped to the first row. He jabbed the pointed end into the ground and rocked the planter slightly to release the right amount of corn. Fitting his step to the space between hills, his pace became rhythmic. He was soon far down the field.

From a tin can I took a handful of kernels and let them drop into a hole I'd dug with my heel. The earth was warm on top and cool beneath. It crumbled like rich piecrust around my feet. When the corn fell it was lost to sight. Had I dropped five or six? At first I couldn't tell, but later my hands knew.

One for the blackbird,
One for the crow.
One for the cutworm,
And two to grow.

Down the long row I chanted Grandpa's planting song. I was proud to drop five, instead of four or six.

The sun grew hot. Clusters of gnats danced infuriatingly before my eyes. The robin's song was ended and the killdeer was quiet. Flocks of blackbirds paced the field and crows assembled in the trees. Grandpa, his back curved, eyes on the planter, moved back and forth across the field, planting four rows to my one.

From the direction of the house sounded a long drawn-out signal. Grandma was blowing the conch shell to call us to dinner. Grandpa laid the planter in the middle of a row and came kitty-cornered across the markings. I set my can in the dirt.

"Hungry?" he asked as he took my hand.

"Starving."

"Tired?"

"No. I love to plant corn."

Grandpa's hand was big and horny, and swallowed mine. I skipped to keep up with him. There was something I wanted to ask. "Grandpa, what would happen if the blackbirds got all the corn? Or the cutworms? What makes them stop?"

He hobbled on in silence, his eyes ahead. I thought he hadn't heard. Then his hand squeezed mine. "They get a tummy ache and can't eat any more. Don't worry, child, there'll always be two to grow."

Grandma

GRANDMA had boiled the huckleberries with sugar. Now she poured them through a funnel into hot jars. Purple juice ran down the sides and she wiped it off with a damp cloth. "There!" she said, when a row of sealed jars gleamed on the table. "And that's just a start. I'll have a hundred jars this season, and maybe that many blackberries." She touched a corner of her apron to her flushed face. "My land, it's hot. Say, could you carry buttermilk out to the field? The men must be dying of thirst."

"Yes, Grandma."

Up from the cellar she brought a pitcher and poured a tin pail full. I walked down a lane bordered with blackberries where an indigo bunting sang from a spray. Papa had told me about buntings and how they nest among thorns. He had sent books with pictures, and his bird paintings hung on our walls at home.

In the hayfield Baron and Big Tom stood hitched to the hay wagon. Grandpa lifted a whole cock of hay from the ground and pitched it onto the towering load. As it came flying, Uncle Lewis caught it on his fork, settled it in place and tramped it down. The team moved ahead. Another forkful sailed upward. The rack was piled high.

"Grandpa!" I hollered as I came near, my hand hurting from the wire bail. I set the pail on the ground and rubbed the red dent in my palm.

"Glory be!" whooped Grandpa. He wiped his face on his bandanna and grabbed the pail. After a long swig he handed it up to Uncle Lewis. When the pail came down it was empty.

"Out of the way, child," said Grandpa. "Wait over there. You can ride back with us in a minute."

A few more forkfuls and the load was built. Grandpa held me up and Uncle Lewis reached halfway and pulled me to the top. I sank into the bouncy hay. "Don't fall off," said Uncle Lewis. "Stay in the middle." He helped Grandpa up. The horses grunted, the wagon creaked, the mountain of hay shivered as though it would fall apart. Grandpa and Uncle Lewis talked and laughed all the way to the barn. "Now scoot," said Grandpa. "You might get speared by a fork."

I ran in to Grandma. She sat in her rocker by the kitchen window, munching raisin cookies and sipping buttermilk. "Want some?" she asked.

"Ugh! Buttermilk's sour."

"Well, have a glass of milk, then, and some cookies." She poured me a glass of sweet milk. When I'd finished eating she said, "I have a surprise for you. Come see." In the hall she pointed to a dim corner under the stairs.

"Kittens," I said.

"Shhhh," she cautioned. "Don't scare her. Just peek." There lay Mittens, Grandma's Maltese cat with seven toes on her front feet. Three kittens were gray like her and the other one, black and white. Their ears were folded down. Their faces were hidden in their mother's fur. "They're nursing," said Grandma. "We won't bother them. Later you can take them out and play."

"Do they have seven toes like Mittens?" I asked.

"I don't know yet. We'll see."

A few weeks later on Sabbath morning I sat in the swing under the grape arbor. Mittens was with me. I could feel the vibrations of her purring as she lay across my lap.

"Hope!" Grandma'd come looking. I wanted to stay there in the cool shade but Grandma wanted me to go to church. "Hope! Where *is* that girl?"

"Here," I called.

Grandma peered in under the grapevines with eyes that blinked from the sun. "Time for church," she said. "Come now, your mother'd have a fit."

"I don't want to go." I jabbed my toe into the dust.

"Why, yes you do," Grandma said. She stepped inside the shade and reached to adjust her hat where a tendril had snatched at the straw.

Church meant knees that hurt on the splintered floor while Brother Jackson yelled at God; high windows that showed just a skimpy bit of the brilliant day outside; and the awful leg-pains from sitting on the flat seat.

"Your mother'd have a fit if I let you stay home," Grandma said. "I know she always takes you."

My toe twisted in the dust. With satisfaction I watched fine powder drift over the shiny patent. I saw the grass stain on one white sock. Yes, Mama made me go. She wanted me to be perfect, but I knew I couldn't be. I felt nearer perfection with Grandma than I did at home. A lot of naughty things happened, but they never seemed so bad when Grandma found them out. I didn't want to leave the swing or let Mittens go.

"Come on, dear. We'll be late."

I looked up. Her eyes smiled into mine. "Do I have to go, Grandma? Can't I stay home this once? I'll be right here with Mittens all the while you're gone."

"Your mother—"

"Please, Grandma."

"Oh, all right. I guess it's no crime to stay home from church—once." She gave her head a defiant toss. With a gloved hand she patted my hair.

At the doorway she hesitated with a sigh.

"What's the matter, Grandma?"

"Nothing, child." She swallowed. "I guess I'm just a failure, that's all." She brushed off a green worm that had let down a thread to her shoulder. Framed in the twining grapevines she gazed out, a sad expression on her face, then she walked out to where Grandpa waited in the buggy.

In the gloom of the arbor the green worm uncurled from the dirt and humped to a post to climb up. Outside a meadowlark called and another answered from far away. The hens in the barnyard clucked and scratched. I heard the buggy wheels turn down the driveway and Prince's footfalls leave the yard, taking Grandma and Grandpa to church. My toes stirred the dust, my hand stroked Mittens' fur and the swing swept to and fro.

One July noon Grandpa sank wearily into his captain's chair and exclaimed, "Dish up, Lib. I'm starving."

Grandma stirred the gravy once more, laid the spoon

aside and poured the gravy into a pitcher. She brought the vegetables and served milk. Grandpa helped himself generously and began to eat. "Worked all morning on that dang stump," he said as he chewed. "Have to get Lafe to dynamite it out."

"Dynamite!" said Grandma. "That'll cost money."

"Yeah, but Lafe'll have it out in a jiffy."

Grandma straightened her shoulders. "How much will it cost, Dar?"

"Nigh on ten dollars. Why?" He peered at her suspiciously.

"Ten dollars! Then let me do it, Dar."

"You crazy, woman?"

"I need almost that much for that washing machine in the Sears catalog. I'd rather work like a mule once for all and not have to scrub clothes every blessed week."

"You're foolish, Lib. You'd waste your time on that stump."

Grandma gave him a look. "I'm going to do it!"

Grandpa pointed his fork at her. "Not a dime if you don't finish the job! And you've only got three days. I want to plow that field."

"All right, Dar."

Grandpa settled in his chair, arms stretched along the rests, while Grandma brought dessert. "Pig-headed female," he grumbled. "Bit off more'n she can chew."

Grandma set squares of gingerbread before us and passed whipped cream.

"You women beat all," Grandpa said as he pitched in. "A machine to wash clothes!" He scraped his plate, wiped his lips and stalked to the living room for his half-hour siesta.

Grandma did the dishes. When Grandpa went out to hitch up his team she said to me, "Come on." A jar of water clutched to her bosom, she marched toward the field where the great pine stump had stood for years next to the huckleberry swamp.

On the way Grandpa drove Big Tom and Baron past us. From high above the rackety mower wheels he looked down and chuckled. "Going on a picnic?"

I whistled to show him I didn't mind.

"Whistling girls and crowing hens always come to some bad end," scolded Grandpa as he drove on.

"I'll show him a crowing hen," said Grandma. She walked faster. Along the lane my bare toes squished dust. We came to the giant stump. Around one side Grandpa had dug a trench, and tangled vines and cut-off roots lay next to pickax, shovel and ax. Grandma gazed from behind her glasses. "Just as I thought. Man's got a one-track mind." She turned to me. "Set the water under that bush. Scat home and bring me a hoe."

"Think you can do it, Grandma?"

"Course I can. If you want to, there's always a way."

When I brought back the hoe she said, "Dar'd never think of using a hoe." She gouged the narrow blade in where a pickax couldn't go and shaved off dirt like cool butter. After she'd dug a pile she backed off and hoed it away. Most of it fell off the blade, so she tried the shovel, but it wouldn't fit between the roots.

"You can't do it," I said.

"Who says?" She got on her knees and scooped up loose dirt with her fingers.

I strolled to the huckleberries and found a few ripe ones. A wood thrush sang, bell-like and slow, deep in the forest beyond. From the distant hayfield came Grandpa's cries of Gee! and Haw! and Consarn you idiots! as Big Tom and Baron tried in vain to please him.

After a while Grandma called me. She sat at the side of the ditch, her skirt pulled to her middle and tied, her gray bloomers damp with dirt. Her white hair was raddled and her glasses askew. "Go home and set the table, child," she said. "When the clock says six, come call me."

I looked at the stump. The hollowed space showed roots aiming straight for China. Grandma knelt, grasped the hoe near its blade and used it like a spoon to scoop dirt. Then she laid the hoe aside, and with curved fingers heaved the sand out between her knees. She squinted up at me. "I watched a she-fox dig a den once, and she went at it just like me. But my hands're a sight bigger than her paws." She smiled through glasses blurred with moisture. "Now get back to the kitchen. Dar'll skin me if supper's not on time."

I had never set the table alone before, but I'd helped Grandma. I arranged the dishes, placed the napkins. From the garden I picked one of Grandma's roses and put it in a glass by her plate. At six o'clock I called her.

"Land sakes, is it time already? I ain't hardly begun." With a grunt she scrambled out of the hole.

At home she hid her dirty dress in the woodshed and tied a fresh apron over the yellow dress she put on. At seven Grandpa sat down. "Get the stump out, Lib?" he asked, with a wink at me.

"Just about," Grandma said pertly.

"You're fibbing," said Grandpa. "Only dynamite'll move it."

"Give me a chance."

Next morning Grandma pinned cut-off black stockings to her sleeves to come down over her wrists. She tied a bandanna over her hair. "Rather roast than itch," she said. "Those horseflies are sinners." At the stump she reared her skirt and pinned it high. "You don't think I can do it, do you?" she asked.

"Well—"

She lowered herself among the half-bared roots. With some dirt dug away they looked vulnerable. "You dig with the hoe, Grandma," I said. "Make a pile of dirt and I'll throw it out."

She looked at my hands, not much bigger than a fox's paws. "To the victors belong the spoils," she declared. "We get this stump out and I'll buy you a new dress."

I tried to scoop dirt as fast as Grandma dug it. Sweat drowned my eyes and salt ran into my mouth. We uncovered root after root but there were always more. The tap root itself was immovably fixed in the ground. "Can't we cut the roots now?" I asked.

"Not yet. I aim to clear the whole thing first so I can chop the tap root like a tree, only upside down." Together we dug like foxes, to make room for an ax to swing. The cool deep earth felt good.

We had gotten to the untouched portion on the far side when Grandma yelled, "Run!" I ran. When I dared look back I saw streaks zipping around Grandma's head as she fled to the huckleberries to brush off a swarm of yellow jackets. I raced home full speed.

Soon Grandma appeared. She stalked to the pump and threw off her dress. "They got me," she said as she tossed water on face and arms. "Here, look down my back, child." No wasps. "Get the baking soda," she said. She plastered a gob of wet soda under one eye, which was tight shut, and poulticed her left arm. She put on the yellow dress and went into the kitchen, with the morning only half gone. She didn't mention the stump. Instead, she started to stir up a batch of doughnuts, a job she took to when upset. "I'll mop the floor when these crullers are done," she said. "I've put on my thinking cap."

While the doughnuts cooled she attacked the floor. I sat on a stool and licked tasty crumbs, wondering what Grandma might do. Swish! Sozzle. Wring. Grandma scrubbed the floor, peering from one eye, her left arm swollen. Dang the wasps!

Suddenly she yelled, "I've got it!" She finished the floor, hung up her apron and went out to hitch up Prince.

"You're going to town," I said. "I want to go."

"Not this time. You stay and keep Mittens company. I'll be right back."

Home in less than an hour, she lifted a burlap bag from the buggy.

"What's in it?" I asked.

"I ain't saying. Magic fades if you tell. Come, help me get dinner on."

At noon, when Grandpa saw her red, swollen face, he guffawed. "Ho! Ho! I told you not to monkey around."

"Darwin Towne, did you know about them wasps?" Grandma's hands were fists.

"I didn't, or I'd have told you." He winked at me. "But they're a good reason why you shouldn't have tackled the job." He stopped eating to grin at her. "I guess now you know you're licked. I'll get Lafe."

"You'll do no such thing! My time's not up. Give me a chance." Grandma jutted her jaw. With one eye shut and her cheek puffed she looked comical, but I didn't join in Grandpa's laugh.

After the dinner hour Grandma bustled to the woodshed and put on her old dress. "You stay home, now," she said, "and don't come snooping. Call me from the pasture gate at six." She heaved the burlap sack over her shoulder and trudged down the lane.

When I called at six, she answered. After a long time she appeared. I'd never seen her so tuckered. At the well I pumped while she splashed water on her balloonlike face. Again she mixed soda with water and spread the cool paste over arm and cheek.

"Did you get the stump out?" I asked.

"Hush, child." She clumped into the kitchen.

At the table Grandpa chewed heartily. "How's them bee stings?" he asked.

"Fine," croaked Grandma.

"How's the stump?"

"Fair to middling."

"You didn't get it out, and you're not going to," said Grandpa. "That'll teach you to mess with man's work."

Grandma lifted her ravaged face. "You think woman's place is rubbing shirts you get filthy dirty," she snapped. "You men have machines to do *your* work."

"Don't manage me, woman." Grandpa waved his fork. "Man's got to do his work the best he can."

"So's a woman! That washer'll do six shirts to a time and wring 'em by turning a crank."

"We can't afford it," said Grandpa.

"You promised me ten dollars. I aim to get it!"

Grandpa muttered something in his mustache and lowered his fork.

Next morning I couldn't wait any longer to find out what Grandma was up to. I circled past the gate and peeked. There stood Grandma in a ditch big as a room, pieces of roots strewn like bones. Her ax hit the tap root with solid blows. Around her a cluster of yellow jackets darted and whined, unable to reach her, for she was encased in a beekeeper's outfit, which she must have borrowed from Stein's apiary. As I stared in admiration I heard her speak crossly: "Go to your young'uns. I moved your nest. Now leave me be."

At noon Grandma came home with the bag on her shoulder. Her hair was wet, her face grimy. She walked bent over. "I did it," she announced almost in a whisper. She threw down the bag and went to the pump.

At the table Grandma confronted Grandpa, her bloated face triumphant. "The stump's out!" she said.

"Humph!" Grandpa glared. Without a word he opened his wallet and handed her a ten-dollar bill. She pounced on it and thrust it in her apron pocket. We ate in silence.

Next morning Grandma hitched up Prince and we drove to town to send off her Sears order. Headed home, we ate ice cream from cones. On my lap I held a new red dress. "I'm plumb wore out," confessed Grandma. "But I feel like kicking up my heels. I'll never scrub clothes again, long as I live."

We exchanged victorious glances as our tongues smoothed the frosty cones.

Mama

IN WATERTOWN, New York, Mama often talked of buying a farm. "I've done it," she said one May evening as we sat down to supper. "I've bought a farm."

I couldn't believe it. Neither could my brothers, Joe and Laurance.

"It's real, all right," said Mama. "I've made a down payment and taken out a mortgage. All we have to do is move. Grandpa will come with his team."

"Will we ride with Grandpa on the wagon?" asked Laurance.

"No, we'll go by train."

"Where is it?" asked Joe.

"About thirty miles from here."

Joe said, "Can I have chickens, Mama?"

"Why, yes. They'll lay eggs for us."

"Can we have a dog?" said Laurance.

"No. A dog's too much trouble, and costs too much to feed."

"I want a cat," I said. "I want one of Mittens' kittens."

"Grandpa can bring a kitten," said Mama.

"About the farm," said Laurance. "Does it have woods?"

"Yes, there's woods and a stream. It has an orchard, and a barn."

"We'll have horses like Grandpa," I said.

"Maybe sometime. Not right away." Mama rose from the table and started to clear the dishes. "You children be good so I can do my work. I've got a lot to think about."

"Will you write Grandpa tonight?" asked Joe.

"Yes. I've got to get packed, too."

Before the first of June we were there. The train had brought us to the town of Vienna, near Oneida Lake, and we'd hired a rig for the half-mile to the farm. The white clapboard house stood under giant maples. Over the porch leaned an ancient locust tree; in the yard syringa and snowball bushes bloomed. I found patches of myrtle and wild strawberry plants in the tall grass.

Mama called from out back. She stood under a row of gnarled lilacs on whose branches leaves had opened. Joe and Laurance bounded around the corner of the house. "Look, children." She gazed upward. "Lilacs! They're one of the reasons I bought the farm. Lilacs right outside my kitchen window!" Her eyes held dreams.

"Another thing's the apple trees. You haven't seen them yet. Come." We walked with her below the barn where a long row of twisted apple trees led in a double line toward the woods. "Look at the blossoms! I've named the farm after those trees—Apple Tree Lane Farm."

In the barn, dry manure still clung to corners of the horse stalls, and remnants of musty hay lay in the mow. On rusty hooks hung odds and ends of harness. While Joe and Laurance explored the chicken coop I stayed in the stable. I pictured my horse in his stall.

"Mama, when will we have a horse?" I asked at supper, which we ate from paper bags, for Grandpa hadn't brought the dishes yet.

"I don't know, dear. I can't afford one now."

"We can have chickens, though," said Joe. "They pay for their keep."

"Finish your supper, children. Grandpa'll be here any minute. We can't go to sleep till he brings the bedsteads and bedding."

After supper we children went to explore the woods. Down the lane under twin rows of apple trees we ran past brushy fields to the woods' edge. We followed an old lumber road through woods of maple, cherry, beech, hemlock and pine, clear to the creek. The stream was too wide for the boys to jump. It flowed silently through swamp grass and water weeds with clumps of alders along its banks. We took off our shoes and socks and dipped our feet.

"Look at the minnows!" shouted Joe.

Laurance said, "Here's forget-me-nots, and jewelweed. I'll bet there'll be cardinal flowers too. They'll bring hummingbirds."

I sat on the bank and extended my feet. Over my legs the water parted with a rushing sound. "See my feet!" I cried. "The water's carrying them away."

Joe and Laurance rolled up their pantlegs and waded in. When water reached their knees they retreated. "I'm going to build a bridge," said Joe. "Then we can cross over."

"We'll make a raft," said Laurance. "We can explore up and down the brook."

It grew dark. We put our socks and shoes back on and walked home. There stood Grandpa's team hitched to the lumber wagon. He and Mama struggled into the house with a mattress. Bed slats and boxes of bedding were still stacked on the wagon.

Grandpa came out. "Joe," he said. "Get that bag from under the seat. Be careful, it's alive."

"My kitten!" I shrieked.

Joe drew out a grain bag with its top tied in a knot. The bottom part moved and a plaintive "Meow" came from within. I could see a bumpy shape. Joe opened the bag and thrust his long arm in. He lifted out a small gray kitten with a white chin, green eyes, and mussed-up fur. Caught in his whiskers were bits of burlap fuzz.

"He's mine!" I reached for him. "Give him to me, Joe."

"Let Hope hold him, Joe," said Mama as she came outside. "You can all play with him, but he's her cat." The kitten snuggled and purred in my arms.

"Take him in the house," said Mama. "Pour some milk, and put a dab of butter on each foot, like Grandma does with Mittens, so he won't run away. He's so young, though, I guess he wouldn't try."

That night my kitten Lally slept on my pillow, purring, his green eyes closed.

Mama made a garden and we helped. But we spent most of our time at the brook. The boys made the raft. It held only one at a time, so we took turns. While they worked on the bridge I got to use the raft all the time. Upstream from the bridge site I poled it along. Schools of minnows darted away from my shadow. Crayfish backed hurriedly into their dens. Yellow and orange jewelweed blossoms nodded on slender stems and the banks were spiked with cardinal flowers, blazing red.

Most days, Mama was away from home. She had found paper-hanging jobs and piano pupils and after doing up the work at home she warned us to be good and walked down the road. While the boys fiddled around near the house I played with Lally and my dolls. When they went to the brook I tagged along. The bridge, made of two logs with boards nailed between, crossed to a maze of brush where catbirds, yellowthroats and thrushes nested. Whenever Laurance found a bird's nest he showed it to Joe and me.

That fall the boys went to school in Vienna. I stayed home with Mama. The boys had pencils, pads, and new books full of pictures. The best book I had was about a rabbit named Ferdinand. The paper covers had worn away and the first page was frayed. I decided to make my book like new. From white shredded-wheat cardboard I carefully cut a cover to fit. Mama let me take needle and thread and showed me how to punch holes with a bigger needle so I could sew the cover on through all the pages. Joe lettered "FERDINAND THE RABBIT" on a paper for me to copy. All one day I worked on cutting and stitching and lettering until the job was done. The book was perfect, and I'd done it myself.

A change happened before spring. Grandpa and Grandma had moved to the outskirts of Vienna, where he had a truck garden and kept Big Tom and Baron. He had sold Prince. He planned to help Mama with the farm and to sell vegetables and work out with his team.

Almost every day, now that spring had come, he drove his team up to our place to plow, harrow and plant. He helped Mama fix the house. They often argued, and Grandpa's voice was loud.

When the first row crops were ready, I helped cultivate. Up on Big Tom, legs spread behind the turrets of the backband, I clutched a rein in each hand. I was supposed to guide the horse so he wouldn't step on young plants. "Giddup," cried Grandpa, as he held the cultivator handles. Big Tom started forward. As his broad back moved I let go the lines and grabbed the turrets. "Whoa!" yelled Grandpa. "Consarn it! You've let him step on the row."

From my height I looked down to see one of Big Tom's hooves mashing a plant. "I can't do it," I wailed.

"Yes, you can. When he goes too far one way, pull him over."

"But I'll fall off."

"No, you won't. Hang on, but watch where he's going." He pulled back on the handles and said, "Back!" Big Tom backed off the row. I set him toward the middle. He started. This time he veered to the other side and stepped on plants again.

"Whoa! Dad blast it, keep him straight," howled Grandpa. "Pull him over before he goes so far." His blue eyes glared. I was frightened at being up so high. I cried.

Grandpa's face softened. "Don't cry, child," he said. "You can do it. Just takes practice." I tried. Grandpa scolded. After a while I could keep Big Tom between the rows all the way and balance myself as he made the turn. I gazed about me from my lofty perch. The bluebirds were at their hole in the apple tree. When we approached their tree the mother bird put her head out to see who was coming. The father flitted ahead of Big Tom, blue wings flashing, warbling as he flew.

Before supper Grandpa hitched up and drove home. There were no horses in our barn. I asked Mama again when we could have a horse.

"If you want a horse, ask your father." Her voice was bitter. "He could get you one if he wanted to."

Mama and Papa did not live together, and Mama supported us herself. Papa was an artist who, I was told, could not make a living, and could not stand family life. He visited about once a year.

"When's Papa coming?" I asked.

She pressed her lips. "I don't know," she said. She stirred the wallpaper paste. The shears and papering brush lay on the kitchen table ready for the next day's job.

"How can I ask him?" I fingered the gluey paste stuck to the big brush.

"Get Joe to write for you."

The paste on the stove thickened, turned from white to lumpy gray. I went out to find Joe. He wrote the letter I dictated: "Please, Papa, I want a horse all my own. I want a pony most of all, but a little horse will be all right. Please, I want him more than anything else in the world." I signed the letter with block letters and added hugs-and-kisses.

I watched the mail for Papa's answer. Each night I prayed for a horse. I cleaned the dried manure out of the stalls, digging into corners with a stick. "Laurance, make me a feedbin," I said. He was in the woodshed at work on his birds'-nest collection.

"Nuts. You haven't got a horse yet."

"But I've asked Papa."

"He's not going to give you any horse."

"Yes, he is. Mama said he might."

"Might. When you get the horse, then I'll build the bin." He took up a leaf cut from paper and painted green. It looked like a real maple leaf, wormholes and all. With thin wire he made a rib and fastened the leaf to a twig of the dry branch mounted on a wooden platform. In the crotch of the branch was a nest.

"What kind's that?" I asked.

"A robin's, stupid. It's from the tree over the porch where the baby birds flew last week. They don't use the same nest twice, so I'm not stealing."

"Wish I could make leaves as good as yours," I said.

"Practice," he said. He daubed a thin line of glue along the center of another leaf and pressed on wire. "You draw pretty good, but you don't do enough of it."

I gazed admiringly at the mounted nests already finished and arranged on a shelf. On one platform a song sparrow's nest lay half hidden in a clump of paper grass.

The letter from Papa finally came. Mama and the boys were in town and Grandpa was in the field mowing. The mower clicked, turned the far corner and came toward me. The blade shuttled fast. "Stand back," yelled Grandpa.

"Wait!" I called. I waved the letter.

Grandpa stopped the horses and wiped his face. "Anything wrong?" he asked, irritably.

"I got a letter. Read it. Please."

"Pshaw! Can't you read yet?"

"Not much. I can't tell what it says."

"Well, get your mother to read it. I've got to cut this

hay." He put his hat back on. "Now get away." He flung out his hand. "Giddup!" he cried. The horses stamped. The mower clicked. Grandpa set his eyes to the standing hay and mowed along.

When Joe came I showed him the letter. He read, "I'm very sorry, but I can't buy you a horse. I wish I could. But it's impossible. Some day I'll tell you why . . ." The letter ended, "With love," and circles and crosses were hugs and kisses.

I put the letter away. With Lally on my lap I sat on the porch and dreamed of riding down the lane and along the road in a saddle, on a swift gray pony with a flowing mane.

Each of us had chores. Joe took care of his chickens and sometimes he let me gather eggs. Laurance split kindling and I helped him fill the woodbox. I set the table and dried dishes and made my bed. My big job was dusting every Friday. We were Seventh-day Adventists, and everything had to be clean and ready for the Sabbath, which was Saturday. I hated to dust.

Morning and evening, no matter how busy, Mama assembled us for worship. After hearing a chapter from the Bible we knelt together to pray. Mama led, and we followed by turn. While the prayers went on and on, my mind jumped from one thing to another. When our prayers were finished we rose, gathered around the piano, and Mama led us in a hymn.

When Mama married she had given up a career in music. She had managed to keep her piano, and no matter what, she kept it in tune. Her alto voice was true, her timing precise. Her blunt, work-roughened fingers kept their dexterity, ranging over the keys with marvelous skill. Mornings, after one hymn, we dispersed to the day's work; evenings, however, especially the long ones in winter, after worship we'd ask her to play. I listened with delight to the rapid glissandos of "Robin's Return," "Spring Song," and the lively Polish mazurkas she knew by heart.

"Those are dance tunes," accused Joe. Dancing was against Mama's religion.

Mama tossed her head. "It's dancing that's wrong; not music. These have lovely rhythm."

When she was weary she played. Her careworn face lifted, her fingers danced like butterflies. "How can you play when you're tired?" I asked her.

"It rests me to play." She smiled. "Playing the piano was my whole life once. Before—Until I met your father." Her eyes met mine, then shifted. "You know, he said I could go on with my music. Art and music together, he said." Her fingers hovered over the keys. "What shall I play?"

" 'Minnehaha,' " I said. She struck the opening chords. Together we shared the anguish of the early settler bereaved by Indian massacre:

> But the laughing Minnehaha,
> Heedeth not the woeful tale.
> What cares laughing Minnehaha
> For the corpse that's in the vale!

She followed with "The Long, Long Trail" and "The Old Red Barn."

"Teach me to play," I begged.

She took my fingers in her stubby hands. "Your fingers're longer than mine were at your age," she said. "I had to stretch my hands till they ached to reach an octave. You have your father's hands. But I don't have time to teach you right now."

In church Mama played the organ for the congregation to sing. Her dark, abundant hair sprang in tiny curls behind her ears. She sat stoutly erect at the organ and her feet trod the pedal for just the right volume. Her voice kept a brisk pace.

One autumn evening Brother and Sister Calvert drove up at dark from their farm down on Fish Creek Flats. Brother Calvert led his big black gelding out to the barn and tied him in an empty stall. He was dressed in clean farm clothes, put on after his day's work. His eyes were deep brown, his hair prematurely gray. He was a deacon, a local pillar, and a fine singer. Mama glowed as she welcomed him and Sister Calvert in for a musical evening.

I was not to share in the music. It was bedtime, the boys already in their room. I slept with Mama in a bedroom across the hall from the living room. After Brother Calvert had bid me a hearty good night and his wife, a quiet lady with pale hair, had given me a hug, I crept off to my bed. Excusing herself, Mama bustled in with the kerosene lamp. "Get right to bed," she said. "The music won't bother you. I'll shut both doors so it won't come through." I wanted to beg to stay up but Mama's rules were like the laws of the Medes and Persians that change not, and it was useless to tease. After a quick kiss Mama left me. Her swift feet crossed the carpet, while the carried light cast weird shadows on the wall until it was cut off abruptly by the shut door. I heard the door on the other side of the hall open and close. I was alone in the silent dark.

For an hour or more I strained my ears to hear the music as it rose in snatches. I caught tantalizing fragments of laughter and talk. I couldn't sleep. Not only was I deathly afraid of the dark, but a bear lived under my bed. I huddled in the middle, covers over my head, my breath stealthy. When I had to get up and use the pot I prayed that Mama would come. I squirmed. The feeling wouldn't go away. "Mama!" I screamed. The singing went right on. "Mama!" I shrieked in a lull of the music. A murmur of voices continued.

I rolled myself into a ball. After a nightmare time a light danced along the curtains and she tiptoed in, a lamp in her hand. She was surprised to find me awake. "Just came to see if you had enough covers." She saw my face swollen from crying. "What's the matter with you?" When I said it was a bear she laughed. "Silly thing." I climbed out of bed to use the pot. Afterwards Mama tucked in the quilts and left. The music resumed; the talk and laughter. I fell asleep.

During Mama's absences we children were alone at home. One day after school Joe lit a fire in the kitchen range and he and Laurance tossed crumpled paper on the hot stove. When the papers burst into flame they dropped them on the wood floor. We all danced around, shouting and singing some ritual stuff from Indian stories. It wasn't suppertime yet. When Mama walked in we were surprised. Hurriedly she put out the flames and quenched our spirits. "I want your solemn promise that you'll never play with fire again."

We promised.

"Now go to your rooms and stay till supper. You'll go without dessert tonight. And while you're in your rooms, think about what you've done and vow to God to do better. Why, you could've burned the house down!"

In our haymow Grandpa had stored extra hay for his team. Soft and springy, it smelled of dried daisies and buttercups mixed with timothy and clover. On a beam high above the hay I crouched as Joe and Laurance climbed the ladder, stood upright and with a wild yell leaped into space, to land in the hay far below. Once in a while Laurance would give me a glance, saying "Come on, fraid-cat. Jump." Or Joe would yell, "Why don't you jump? You're a coward."

Joe climbed the ladder and stood tall above me. "I'm going to push you," he said.

I clung in terror. "Don't touch me. I'll tell Mama."

"Tattletale! Why don't you jump? You're missing the fun."

"I'll jump when I get ready."

With a screech he leaped forward. Laurance followed him down.

I stood up, and grasped the upright timber. My legs trembled, my head felt giddy. The hay was a long way down. Laurance swarmed up the ladder, brushed past me and flung himself into space. He landed, unhurt, and as he lay sprawled I got up courage. "Look out!" I shouted. I jumped. My breath was gone; my heart in a knot. I hit the hay with bent knees and flopped over—laughing. After that first jump the rest was easy.

When we got tired of jumping Joe had an idea. "Let's climb to the barn roof," he said to Laurance. "From there I bet you can see all over the farm." They put up the ladder and its tip touched the eaves. "You hold it steady," Joe told Laurance. He started to climb. At the eaves he gripped the shingles and clambered off the ladder to creep up the slanted roof on hands and knees.

"Hold the ladder," said Laurance to me. He reached the top rung and crawled after Joe. I stood back to watch.

Joe had reached the peak. One leg on each side, he rose from his knees, hands on the ridgepole, then stood straight, stretching out his arms. He took a step. Soon he was at the far end. "I can see Baker's house," he bragged. "If the woods weren't there I could see clear down to Raut's."

Now Laurance straddled the ridgepole. He walked slowly, arms straight out. My heart was in my mouth when he stumbled. The boys laughed and shouted. After a while I got bored. "What'll Mama say?" I yelled.

They looked at the lowering sun. "We'd better get down," said Joe. "If Mama comes home early she'll catch us."

"She's never told us not to climb the roof," said Laurance.

"She said not to get into mischief," I reminded them.

"Who says it's mischief?" asked Laurance. "Besides, she doesn't have to know. Don't you tattle now."

I held the ladder while they climbed down. They put it back in its place. Joe and Laurance brought big armloads of wood and I set the table for supper.

Mama was quiet when she came in. She tied an apron over her dress and prepared supper with scarcely a word. After supper she told us, "Come in the other room." When we got there she said, "Sit down."

"Now," she said, facing the boys, "tell me what you did today."

The boys told of their chores and of our fun in the hay.

Mama looked grim. "Boys, I have something to tell you," she announced. "Today while I was at work, God showed me what you were up to."

We three looked at each other, gripped by mystery.

"You don't know the power of God," she went on. "He has ways of helping parents look after their children, and His ways are past finding out." She paused for that to sink into our souls. Then she added, "God showed me you boys climbing up that barn roof, walking along the ridgepole. Why, you might have broken your necks! Don't you ever do anything like that again!"

We were aware that God knew everything, but this was the first hint that He might tell on us. The boys sat stunned, their feet pushed against the legs of their chairs.

The Naturalist

It was a bright May morning. We'd been on the farm a year and I was five. Robins were building in the maple near the porch, where I played with my kitten and my dolls. I saw the mother robin bring a beakful of dry grass to the half-finished nest. She sat, then moved around to shape the inside of the nest. She flew away, and before long returned with a beakful of mud, which she worked into the nest. Soon she would be laying eggs.

A crunch came on the gravel of the driveway. A tall man walked briskly along the side of the house. Under his shabby hat his eyes glowed in a face that was dark and lean. On his back he carried a frayed knapsack. In his left hand he held a book, and in his right a small square package.

As he strode with Indian swiftness along our driveway I shrank into a corner. He was a stranger and I was afraid. He went on past and I heard his fist hammering on the back door. Then came the sound of the opened door and Mama's voice.

His footfalls crossed the grass to the porch. When he saw me he smiled, leaped up the steps and threw out his arms, saying, "Hello! Aren't you glad to see me?"

Papa was here! I hadn't seen him since we'd moved from the city. Now he would take me to the woods and tell me more secrets of nature, which he had done sometimes on Grandpa's farm. He would play games and tell stories, and best of all, he would draw me pictures of animals.

As he rushed up, Lally streaked across the floor and shot up a post to disappear behind a rafter. "You scared my kitten," I cried.

"Don't worry. I'll get him." He stepped nimbly to the rail and reached to the rafter. "Come kitty, come kitty," he said. He poked with his hand. "He's too far back, but he'll come out later." He came near me. "Aren't you going to ask what I've brought you?"

"What've you got, Papa?"

"Here's a book."

I took it. It was thin. On the front was a picture of a tulip tree with bright orange blossoms and a bumblebee striped in yellow and black. I turned the pages and saw more pictures. "Thank you," I said.

"And look here." He held up a package. "What do you say?"

For a moment I was puzzled, then I remembered the game we had played at his last visit. "Gimme!" I cried.

He unwrapped the box and held it out. "I know a little girl who's got the gimmes," he said, eyes atwinkle.

"Candy's the only cure." While I ate the candies he became my father again.

"Want to go for a walk?" he asked. He took my hand and led me toward the woods. As we passed the kitchen window I saw Mama peering past the curtain. She was already part of another world.

Down the lane I skipped beside him. He told me the steeplebush lining our path was called hardhack because of its tough stems. From the meadow came a bobolink's song. "He's singing to his mate," Papa said. "She's deep in the grass near that tall weed he's on, sitting on brown-speckled eggs."

We reached the woods, where trees spread partial shade. There was still frost in sheltered spots. The air was warm, however, and I pulled off my shoes. My toes sank into moss and my feet felt dry leaves. Beside a rotting log he showed me a clump of red wake-robin and a cluster of green May apples with their umbrella-like leaves. "Listen," he said, and identified the trill of a migrating warbler high in a maple. "Look." He stooped to pick up a wood frog. He put the smooth frog into my hand. "Hold him close to the ground," he said. The frog was maple sugar trimmed with chocolate. He sat still on my palm, his pale throat moving in and out. When he leaped he landed far away, then leaped again.

As we passed a huge beech tree a big brown bird whirred up, her wings scattering leaves. She curved away through the trees. "A grouse," my father said. He walked nearer the tree, leaned over and pushed aside the leaves. As though his hands had painted a picture, he revealed a grouse's nest. Nestled in a bed of leaves lay a dozen pale brown eggs. The mother's tawny feathers had kept them hidden while she brooded. Her whirring flight had covered them with leaves. The eggs lay like freckled mushrooms in their leaf-lined hollow. "I want one," I said.

"No. Don't ever take an egg from a bird's nest. That's worse than stealing from people."

I clasped my hands and looked. From deep in the forest came the cry of the mother, calling us away from her nest. We turned and tiptoed off, out to the field, while the mother grouse still cried from the depths of the woods. I put my shoes on and we walked back to the house.

"I'll be busy this afternoon," my father said as he left me at the kitchen door. "But I'll be back after supper. We are going to another place—to hear the woodcock sing."

At the table I jabbered to Mama about the wood frog, the bololink and the grouse's nest. "Eat your dinner," she said. Before I was through she had risen and begun doing the dishes. "I've got bread to bake and two batches of cookies to roll out," she said. Silently I finished and went out to the porch. I petted my kitten. I looked at the pictures in the new book, but I kept seeing the grouse's nest. My palm still felt the surge of the frog's leap to freedom. Red wake-robin bloomed before me, along with green crowns of May apples among weathered leaves. I longed to make pictures of them all.

After supper I went out and sat in the swing to watch the sun. As it left the treetops Papa came. We walked down a trail through dense cedars to a clearing next to the creek. A rosy afterglow filled the west.

"The woodcock will sing," he whispered. No sooner had he said it than a harsh "Peent!" sounded among the scattered weeds and brush of the clearing. "Peent! Peent!" The notes came from the ground. Before each call there was a gurgle like liquid running out of a bottle.

"Where is he?" I whispered.

"Sh-h-h." Papa pressed my hand. "Wait."

The long-beaked bird flew almost straight up, then circled. He rose higher and higher till I could no longer see him. "He's gone," I said.

My father still gazed skyward. "He'll come down singing."

A faint twitter came from the sky. "He's throwing himself back and forth up there, singing," my father said. "Listen, he's coming down."

Still singing, the bird spiraled downward. He twittered, trilled and chortled before he plummeted to earth. Once more he called from the ground, then rose again for his serenade in the sky. When darkness came my father picked me up and carried me home.

The next morning he was back. This time he took me to the orchard, where I showed him the nesting bluebirds. As we sat on a stone wall he took from his pocket paper and pencil and asked, "What do you want me to draw?"

"A kitten." Swiftly he sketched a kitten playing with a ball.

"A horse." He drew a running horse, legs bunched for speed. "You didn't finish him," I said, pointing to the broken lines of the sketch.

He laughed. "You're right." He drew in the missing lines.

"Draw a bird," I said. He drew a robin, put him on a branch and surrounded him with leaves.

"Draw the bluebirds, Papa." He sketched the male on

a twig, the female peeking from the hole in the gnarled apple trunk.

For several days we were together outdoors. He never went in the house or talked with Mama. He stayed at the farm next door.

One morning he arrived with his knapsack strapped on. He sat on the porch steps and took me on his knee. "I'm going away," he said. "Out West. I won't see you for a long time."

"Why, Papa?"

"I don't know." His fingers clutched at his knee as he stared across the yard to the old apple tree where the bluebirds lived. He turned to me, caught both my hands in his and said, "I'll write. I'll send you souvenirs. Look for little packages in the mail. You write me, too, and draw me pictures." He stood up. The stubble of his beard scratched my cheek. His arms hurt my ribs. Then he wheeled and marched away, tall and straight beneath the knapsack.

In the kitchen Mama dropped dough for cookies into a pan. "Papa's gone," I told her. "Why did he go away?"

"I don't know." Each gob of dough made a peaked mound. "Here, take this spoon and spread the cookies," she said. "Dip it in water so it won't stick."

My heart ached with the question, "Why?"

Tom

AT THE EDGE of the woods Laurance and Joe made a house of trees. A group of cedars grew so close that their branches intermingled. With a hatchet the boys trimmed branches to form a window facing the pasture. The dense green needles formed the sides of the house. Other branches were hacked off to form a doorway through which we stooped into a dim interior. On logs we sat to look out our window while bluejays called in the treetops and towhees scratched the duff. Out the window we could see across feathery spires of hardhack and tangles of blackberries clear to the barn. Around our woodland house flourished gardens of white violets nestled at the base of tall ferns.

One Friday night at sunset we persuaded Mama to walk down with us. Her Sabbath dress caught on briars; her shoes grew dusty. But she liked the house. She squeezed through the low doorway and said, "Look at the sunset out that window!" From her dress pocket she drew forth a Bible. "We'll have evening worship right here."

She read the verse about "in My house are many mansions," and reminded us that the woods, the sky and the flowers were but a shadow of the riches God had prepared in heaven, if we would renounce our sins and do what was right. "Let us pray," she said, closing the Bible. We knelt on the soft brown carpet and took part in the ritual that welcomed the Sabbath each week.

For me, Sabbath was irksome. The only fun was to be dressed in clean clothes that I could show off at church. The boys looked strange in good pants and shoes, with caps on well-combed hair. We walked all together along the dirt road, down Baker's Hill, along the flats to Rauts' and then past one house after another to the church around the corner.

The church building was a schoolhouse during the week. On Sabbath it looked different, with rigs hitched under the shed, grownups in the yard and standing on the steps. Joe and Laurance joined a group of rowdy friends in the back row. Opposite them sat Elder and Sister Ledstetter, ready to shush them, or to intervene if spitballs should start to fly. The Ledstetters were our most respected members for they had a daughter married to a foreign missionary and their son was an ordained minister in another state. They were considered oracles because they had raised exemplary children. Elder Ledstetter's deep-set eyes never smiled behind his round-lensed owl's glasses in his broad, wrinkled face. His grim mouth was ready to warn, "Stop that!"

He was not my problem, for I stuck close to Mama up

front, where she sat to be near the organ. When the congregation divided into classes I left Mama to go upstairs with a group of girls my age. Sister Scanley was our teacher. Like Elder Ledstetter, she had big round glasses. Hers slid far down her thin nose. Fly-away gray hair outlined her monkey face. She held her Bible in both hands and closed and opened it nervously as she said, "All right, girls—" Whispers and giggles continued. She cleared her throat. "Now, girls—" After a while the boisterousness quieted and she started to read the day's text. No matter what the text, her talk ended with a warning that God punishes those who remain sinful.

While Sister Scanley's voice went on and on I looked out the window. Far through the trees gleamed Miller's pond where we skated in winter and fished in summer. A bittern lived there, and in spring red-winged blackbirds called. I twisted my feet around the legs of my chair to ease the crawly feeling that made me want to kick and jump.

In spite of how I felt about church, I longed to go to school. Mama said, "Wait till you're seven." Something happened first, however, to make me forget school.

The First World War was over. Returned from war, without jobs, men traveled the roads. Many were tramps in frayed clothing, packs on their backs or bundles in their hands. In addition, salesmen peddled from town to town. Some came by train, put up at a hotel and hired a rig to canvass the territory. Others drove their own rigs.

One day a buggy-riding salesman dropped in and stayed to supper. He was a genial man who told a hard-luck story. Mama invited him to stay overnight. He unhitched his bay horse and put a halter on him so he could graze. "Want to hold him?" he asked me. "He's perfectly gentle. A child can walk right under him." He put the rope in my hand, stepped to the horse's side. "Whoa, Tom," he said, and stooped under the horse's belly. He patted Tom and slipped back under. Tom kept on cropping the long spring grass.

"Gentle as a kitten," said the man.

"Let me hold him," said Joe. He made a grab for the rope.

"He told me to," I said, and hung on.

"Take turns," said Laurance. "I want to hold him too."

I watched Tom's muscles ripple under his sleek coat and saw the skillful way he handled the grass. His nose found choice bunches, his lips closed, and with a sideways jerk his teeth snipped them off. Still chewing, he moved on. His tail was long, and gleaming black. His forelock almost covered his eyes. I saw a patch of white peek from a part in his forelock. "He's got a star!"

Later the salesman led Tom to the barn. From the back of the buggy he pulled a bag of oats and dumped a big feed into the box. "That's his supper," he said. "Your supper's ready, too, your mother said. Let's go in."

At the table we talked about Tom and how he was not a biter and kicker like Grandpa's Prince, but loved children. Mama and the horse's owner exchanged glances.

In the morning I went to the barn early. From far back I talked to Tom. He gave a whinny as though answering me. Joe and Laurance bounded in. They led him out to graze. When the man appeared he said, "How's your horse this morning?"

In the kitchen Mama said, "God has sent us a horse. I've bought Tom."

After breakfast the man took a pack from the buggy and a battered suitcase. "Can't afford to keep a horse," he said. "I know he'll have a good home with you."

Grandpa mended the fence. Tom stayed in the pasture when he wasn't working, but he was busy most of the time. Mama had bought him so she could give more piano lessons and do more papering. She could now go ten miles or more to a job. She let us ride Tom while he fed in the yard, but not anywhere else. "He's got to save his strength," she said.

She had to be away so much that she decided I could go to school that fall, although I was only five. She hitched up Tom that first day and drove us.

Our teacher, Miss Gifford, wore a starched white blouse with round collar. Pinned to it was a watch like a gold teardrop. Her hair was a high, loose pompadour.

We first graders were in front of the second graders. Behind them was third, then fourth, back to big boys and girls in the eighth grade.

I longed to read, and here were books galore. Stacks of them stood on the floor beside Miss Gifford's desk. She called us to order and wrote our names. "I have your school supplies," she announced. "Now, before I give you these I want to tell you how to treat books. Don't open a new book flat all at once." She took a volume, stood it on its spine, and separated a few pages at the front. "Open it like this," she said. "These books were bought for you by the church. You must take good care of them." She handed out books, paper and pencils. My speller was red, my reader green, arithmetic blue. The pad had ruled lines. The yellow pencil was already pointed. When I reached my seat I began to scribble.

"Attention, boys and girls," Miss Gifford said. "Do not write anything yet. I will assign your first lesson. Then write only what is required for that lesson." She called the eighth graders up front first to assign their lessons, while the rest of us opened our books. My green-backed reader was full of pictures. I went through it, page by page. I wanted to copy a certain picture from my reader. It was of an apple cut in half with the pattern of the seeds exposed. A line ran from the stem, around the seeds and down. It was the most beautiful picture I had ever seen. My hand squeezed the pencil. In the space below the block letters on my pad I copied the picture, with light lines at first, as Papa had taught me, until the shape was right. Once the outline was sure I pressed down hard. On the stem of my apple I added a leaf with a worm hole in it.

I had barely finished the picture when Miss Gifford said, "It's ten minutes to four. Put your things in your desk neatly. Leave finished work on top of your desks." She walked down the aisle and collected the papers. On my desk lay the single sheet with the picture on. She took it up without a word and added it to the sheaf on her arm. "School's dismissed," she said. We rushed pell-mell for the door. We detoured by Miller's pond, then went crosslots through Raut's pasture. We passed through the meadow and on to the gravel-pit grown up to weeds and saplings and blackberry bushes. Snakes lived there among piles of stones. In the bushes catbirds, song sparrows and brown thrashers had nested, and in the crotches of young trees, goldfinches. These summer birds were still around, silent now except for an occasional chirp.

In a certain burrow guarded by a boulder lived a

woodchuck. When we appeared he raised his head and ran to the mound before his hole. There he sat to watch us. When we moved close he dived with a chirrup. Past the gravel pit we came to Baker's orchard. Robins' nests sat on the branches, oriole nests hung from drooping limbs and bluebirds still flew about the orchard where they had raised their broods in rotted-out branches and woodpecker holes.

The days were short and the sun was almost set before we reached home. We crawled under our pasture fence and raced up the lane. Mama wasn't home yet, but we knew what to do. Joe went to feed his chickens, Laurance to clean Tom's stable, and I to feed Lally and set the table.

That evening after dinner there was a difference. I too was a pupil, with books and pad. At one end of the long library table I settled down to draw the apple picture again, on the white back of flour-bag paper. Mama saved the 50-pound flour sacks for us. If they were wrinkled she ironed them before she cut them into sheets and stacked them neatly in the cupboard.

"You don't know how lucky you are," she said when we complained because paper was scarce. "Abraham Lincoln had only a board to write on. And no kerosene lamps, only light from the fireplace." I filled my sheets with pictures to the very edge.

Mama hummed softly as she mended socks. Joe and Laurance sprawled at each side of the table, their books scattered, as they did their lessons. I tried in vain to get the apple picture right.

"What's the matter?" said Laurance when I groaned.

"I can't get it right," I said. "It doesn't look like the one in the book." He came to lean over my shoulder. "Look, yours is better than the book. Yours is uneven, like a real apple. And that worm hole in the leaf is good." Comforted, I began to color the picture. When it was done I showed it to Mama. "That's nice," she said. She folded a darned sock and rose from her chair. "Time for bed, children. Go brush your teeth."

I showed the picture to Laurance. "It's fine," he said. "Colors are good." He slammed his book and made for the kitchen to get to the sink first.

The next day Miss Gifford handed back my paper with a big red A in the corner. She didn't scold me about the picture. When the day's work was done I colored the apple and did better than I had at home.

Winter came early, with snow before Thanksgiving, and the snow stayed. We took our sleds to school. At the top of Baker's Hill we flung ourselves down, belly-whacker, and coasted clear to Raut's. At recess we played fox-and-geese and at noon we had time to cross the road and slide down Elder Ledstetter's hill back of his barn. It was a short, steep hill that ran right under the barbed wire fence into his cow pasture.

One day Alex Turner, a fourth-grader, raised his head going down and gashed his face on the wire. Blood ran down over his scarf and soaked the snow. Ernie Fields rushed to bring Miss Gifford. We all went with her as she led Alex to the schoolhouse. From the cabinet she took iodine, cotton and bandages. Soon Alex had a white bandage across his forehead and down one cheek. Miss Gifford gave us a lecture. "Boys and girls, I know Elder Ledstetter's hill is the only one close enough. I hate to say you can't go there. Don't let anything like this happen again, or I'll have to say no."

Back at the fence Laurance noticed something. "Hey, look," he yelled. "This bottom wire's sagging. I'm going to take the wire off—or loosen it and lift it up. I'll ask Elder Ledstetter."

"I bet the old skinflint won't let us slide here if we meddle with his fence," said Ernie.

"I'll promise to fasten it back before the cows are out in spring," said Laurance. He went up on the Ledstetter porch. I went with him, staying in back. Elder Ledstetter opened the door a crack and stared with his owl's eyes. "What you want?" he asked crossly.

"Sliding under the fence we might hit the wire and get hurt," said Laurance. His mittened hands were clenched behind his back. "Could I take out the staples and lift the bottom strand, just until spring? I'd put it back."

Elder Ledstetter glowered, one hand on the knob, the other holding a paper he'd been reading. He lifted his eyes to the barn lot, where kids were shuffling in the snow, holding the ropes of their sleds. "Well, I guess so." He looked Laurance straight in the eye. "If any of my cows get out, you school children'll never use that hill again."

After that we had a two-foot leeway and could even go down sitting up if we flipped backward a second before the wire could hit.

Mama clothed us in double mittens and full-length wool stockings she knit herself. Snow soaked our mittens, and got inside our overshoes. At four o'clock when we started home the sun was already low. By the time we got home we were freezing.

One afternoon I walked home in a blizzard. My hands ached. I held my dinner pail in one hand, books under my coat, while I beat the other hand against my knee. Joe and Laurance trudged ahead; I followed in their tracks. My legs grew heavy and my feet felt like blocks of wood. Finally my hands stopped aching. I couldn't see in the swirling snow, but the boys knew where to turn in. I stumbled through the door into the kitchen. Mama said, "Boys, shake your hats and coats out on the porch. Brush the snow off your overshoes before you come in." She turned to me where I stood with arms pressed to my sides. "Here, I'll help take off your things." She removed my red tuque, frosted with snow, and dropped it on the floor. "Take off your mittens." She knelt to unbutton my coat. "What's the matter?" she said when she saw my screwed-up face. "Can't you move?"

I saw Mama's exasperation change to concern as she took my right hand in both hers and tried to budge the dinner pail. My fingers wouldn't let go. Gently she pried them loose, worked my mitten off over the bent fingers, then slid off the other mitten. The mittens were stiff as clothes hung on a winter line; my fingers were white icicles.

Joe and Laurance clumped back in. "Her fingers're frozen," Mama told them. "Laurance, go pump me a basin of cold water. Joe, change your clothes and go do the chores. You do Laurance's, too; he's got to stay and help me."

She worked my coat off one arm at a time. On a kitchen chair far from the stove she had Laurance put the basin. She seated me next to it and plunged both my hands in. "Keep your hands right down in that water," she commanded. "They mustn't feel heat till they're thawed." She spoke to Laurance. "You stay beside her and see she doesn't pull her hands out. As the frost leaves her hands they are going to hurt. Tell her stories or something."

Laurance gripped my wrists. He began a story about the rabbit who lost his tail. At first my hands didn't feel. When they woke up they started to ache. I writhed and tried to pull my hands away, and cried aloud. As the pain increased I shrieked. Laurance's blue eyes were soft but his grip was iron.

"Hush!" said Mama. "The neighbors will hear you."

"Don't cry," begged Laurance. "I'll give you a whole handful of marbles—my best glassies."

Joe stamped in, covered with snow. "I could hear you clear out in the barn," he said. He came and stood near while he took off his mittens. Through my tears I saw pity change his face. "Know what I'll do?" he said. "I'll give you fifty cents if you stop crying."

I tried. But the pain wouldn't let me. For an hour I screamed and struggled, and begged Laurance to let me go. When Mama saw color in my fingers she took them out and dried them on a towel. She drew a chair from the table, where supper was set, and massaged them in her plump warm hands. She fed me with a spoon. Afterwards, when we were gathered in the living room while the blizzard roared outside, Laurance got out his cigar box and picked a handful of red, blue and green marbles. To them he added three of his best glassies, including the one I envied most—crystal clear with a glistening red spot inside.

Meanwhile, Joe had brought something in his closed

fist and put it in my lap. It was a fifty-cent piece, the first I had ever had. "But you said—if I stopped crying," I said.

"I know. But you tried, didn't you?"

Mama sat at the piano and played and sang softly while the boys did their homework.

The winter continued cold. One white morning with the temperature below zero Mama said she'd take us to school in the pung. Uncle Lewis lived with us then, logging in the woods. He hitched up Tom and drove to the door. Tom's breath issued like steam. He snorted and pawed the snow. The thills of the pung groaned. "He's rarin' to go," said Uncle Lewis. "I don't think you can hold him."

"Yes, I can," said Mama. She wound a heavy scarf around her neck and pulled on thick wool mittens. "Tom's never run away." She tucked us snugly under the buffalo robe while Uncle Lewis held Tom's bridle. My wool tuque was jammed low over my eyebrows and my scarf covered the end of my nose. The air bit my face. Tom fizzled like a firecracker.

Mama took the lines firmly in her mittened hands. "All right," she told Uncle Lewis. He let go and jumped aside. Tom shot ahead; we swerved out the driveway on one runner and flew down the road. Tom's hoofs squeaked on the hard-packed road and the runners sang. We flashed past the frozen orchard, the gravel pit and the snow-buried meadow. Mama kept tight hold on the lines as we dashed through town. At the side street on which the school stood she tried to slow down, but Tom wouldn't slow. He turned the corner sharp and hurled himself, full gallop, toward the school. He knew the shed was there, and made a beeline for its shelter.

Desperately Mama sawed on the lines. We all hollered, "Whoa!" but Tom had the bit in his teeth. He rounded the front of the schoolhouse, veered suddenly, and the pung overturned, flinging us into the snow.

Mama scrambled to her feet, brushed snow off us and helped find our dinner pails. She went to the shed, where Tom stood meekly, to put the robe back in the pung.

No one was hurt. Nothing was broken. But a special treat of peach pie Mama had packed for our dinner had sailed into a drift and it stayed there until spring.

Fluffy

April of the next spring was marked by the ordeal of Fluffy. The boys each had a cat now: Laurance a yellow tabby named Stripes; Joe a gray Angora named Fluffy. I still had Lally. Each of us had to take care of his own cat. Though I loved Lally, there was something special about Fluffy—her long silky hair.

One day Fluffy disappeared. Joe and Laurance and I went all over the farm, calling. "She's wandered off, but she'll be back when she's hungry," said Mama. "She's just got spring fever."

A week went by. Fluffy never answered our calls. On Sabbath morning we walked to church, dressed in our best. "Boys," called Mama as Joe and Laurance raced across the ditch into the orchard. "Stay on the road. You'll spoil your clothes. Walk quietly; you're on your way to church."

I skipped ahead, the feel of April sunshine warm on my hair, the dusty road against my feet. Snow still lay along the ditches in dirt-speckled drifts, but a breeze from the east brought scents of early flowers and sun-warmed earth. "Hope, come back here. Don't skip on the Sabbath. And I want you to be quiet in church, too. No dessert for dinner if you don't behave."

As we passed the gravel pit Joe cried, "Stop!" He turned to face the field. "Listen," he said. A faint meow came from the gravel pit.

"Fluffy!" He dashed into the gravel pit, Laurance after him. I ran too. The briars raked my good coat; the weeds scratched my legs. When I came to Joe and Laurance they were kneeling beside the woodchuck hole. Something lay on the ground—something gray, with thick matted fur. It was Fluffy. I smelled a strange odor. Fluffy's left hind foot was caught in a trap. The curved jaws cut into mangled flesh turned gray.

"Help me get this trap off," said Joe to Laurance. "Put your foot on the spring. Be careful. Don't step on her foot." Laurance placed his Sabbath shoe on the strong spring and grabbed my shoulder for balance. Joe pried the jaws apart. Fluffy was free. She mewed feebly. Joe cradled her in his arms while Laurance kicked the stake loose and picked up the trap. We came out to Mama.

"I've got to take her home," said Joe.

Mama touched Fluffy. "We'll all go home," she said. "The Bible says a man must rescue an ox fallen into a pit, even on the Sabbath."

"Or a cat caught in a trap," said Laurance.

Too weak to stir, Fluffy lay in Joe's arms. "It's a miracle you heard her," said Mama to Joe. "She was too far gone to cry loud."

"We passed right by here every day," Joe said. "Why didn't we hear her before?"

Mama sniffed the air. "Wind's from the east. You wouldn't have heard her with it the other way."

"It's a miracle that she mewed just when we got here," I said.

"No, silly," said Laurance. "She heard us talking and called for help."

"That's right," said Mama.

At home she cooled boiled water from the teakettle and with a clean rag bathed Fluffy's leg while Joe held her. "Gangrene's set in," Mama said, her face grim, as she wiped away rotten flesh and fragments of fur. The smell was sickening.

"What's gangrene?" I asked.

Laurance answered. "Stupid, it's where part of the body dies from lack of blood. That trap's been on a week. Her foot's dead. That's what you smell."

"Give me the peroxide," said Mama, as she dropped the wet cloth into the water. Laurance handed her the brown bottle. "Hold her over the pan," she said to Joe. The cork came out with a pop and she tipped the bottle. The burning medicine drenched Fluffy's leg and fizzed up. I squirmed. I knew how it stung. Fluffy didn't seem to mind. She can't feel, I thought. Her leg's dead.

"Stop fidgeting, Hope," said Mama. "Go in the pantry and get milk for this cat. Put bread in." I poured a bowl of milk and crumbed in bread.

With pieces of old sheet Mama bandaged Fluffy's leg lightly. "Not too tight," she explained. "Air's got to get to the wound." Joe put a flannel rag in a box behind the stove and laid Fluffy down. She wouldn't touch the bread and milk.

"That's the best we can do," said Mama. "Be thankful we found her." She emptied the basin and rinsed the cloth. "It's too late for church," she said. "But we've done a good deed. The righteous man regardeth the life of his beast. Come on in the living room and we'll have our own Sabbath school, right here at home."

She read the story of the Good Samaritan.

"We're Samaritans, aren't we, Mama?" I interrupted. "We took care of Fluffy when she was left by the road to Damascus."

"—to Vienna," said Laurance, and he and Joe tittered.

"Hush," reproved Mama. "It's no joke. Jesus said, Unto the least of these. Fluffy is small, but in helping her we've shown mercy. Blessed are the merciful, the Bible says."

Joe, serious once more, added, "Not a sparrow shall fall." As we knelt in prayer, each of us, beginning with Mama, expressed thanks for Fluffy's rescue.

The moment prayers were over we children rushed to the kitchen to see how Fluffy was. She lay stretched flat, her breath coming in gasps. Foul-smelling liquid oozed through the white bandage and stained the flannel.

"Leave her alone," said Mama. "Joe, put wood on the fire. Laurance, you go down cellar and bring up food. Hope, set the table for dinner."

"Fluffy won't eat," I said.

"She's too tired and sick right now. Let her rest."

By suppertime Fluffy had revived a little. She lapped a few drops of milk, then sank back. Before bedtime she ate a bit of bread and milk. In the morning we found that she'd wormed the bandage off and dragged herself near the door.

"We must take her out twice a day," said Mama. "She wants to be clean."

"What about the bandage?" asked Joe.

"We'll leave it off. She'll lick her wound and do it more good than medicine."

Fluffy ate more and more. She spent hours licking her leg. One day when I came home from school Fluffy's foot was gone.

"It had to come off," said Mama. Calmly she reached pans from a high shelf. "Her foot was making her sick. She'll heal better now."

"How'd you do it?"

"With the ax."

"You hurt her!" I accused.

"Her foot was numb," she said. She ran grease around the cupcake pans. "She couldn't feel—like the time your hands were frozen, before they started to thaw."

Fluffy licked the stub of her leg.

Joe and Laurance came in. "Mama cut off her foot," I told them.

"Now she'll get well," said Joe.

The stump healed. The smell went away. With her old enthusiasm Fluffy groomed her fur until it became soft and shiny again and her tail plumed out. She learned to walk on three feet. The rusty trap, jaws closed, hung in the barn.

Second Grade

It was an evening in September, with gusts of wind rattling the shutters. Laurance was doing fifth-grade arithmetic and I had my grade two reader in front of me. My eyes traveled around the kitchen with its seven doorways. Only the living room and parlor doors were open and they showed solid blackness. Mama and Joe had gone down to Grandpa's. Laurance and I were alone. Under the chair my feet were drawn up onto a rung as I sat between two fears. One was terror that things would come out of the dark. The other was dread that Laurance would see my fear.

Suddenly he whacked his book shut. I gave a jump. "See? You're afraid," he said. "You're always scared when Mama's gone."

"No, I'm not," I said fiercely.

"All right, smarty." He sat back with his closed book in his hands. "Prove it. You know that old biddy's been setting in the barn? Go bring me one of her eggs."

I couldn't go to the barn alone—at night. I couldn't even pass through the back room to the toilet without Mama carrying a light and leaving Lally with me. Tom was out to pasture and the barn was empty except for the old hen.

Laurance's hands were hard and brown, his knuckles rough. On his fingers were many scars. "Well, are you going?" he asked. "The old hen won't hurt you. Might peck a little."

"I—I—" My tongue was too big for my mouth and my throat was dry. He'd call me fraidy-cat. "I'll go," I whispered. Laurance opened his book and jotted figures. As I rose from the chair my legs had licorice whips for bones and my feet were numb. I moved slowly, with the hope that Laurance would relent. "Be sure to bring the egg," he said without looking up.

Out the door I went into the black night. Strange figures took shape all around. Ahead was a shaggy bear, which changed into the tall pine near the well as I came closer. The barn door hinges whined as I entered. The old floor creaked. It was dark in there—dark as the cellar when the lantern's gone out. As my feet stumbled into the straw of the stable a mouse skittered away. I listened for a long time, the beat of my heart like a clock in my head.

A rustle came from the manger. My neck prickled. One—two—three—four. I took the last steps to the manger. My hand touched smooth feathers, and a sleepy murmur came from the hen. She gave a squawk when I clutched a warm egg and drew it out. She fluffed her feathers and tried to tuck the egg back under. Ouch! She had pecked my wrist.

I wanted to run back to Laurance. Instead, I carried the egg firmly in both hands. At the door of the barn something soft settled over me like a net over a butterfly. I clung to the egg while my heart pounded. It was only a bunch of cobwebs jarred from the beam overhead. I brushed it off and opened the door, to immense blackness. Over on the woodpile something moved. My legs melted. I remembered a story Mama had read to us, of Molly Pitcher carrying water while bullets whizzed past. Why couldn't I be brave like her?

A dark blob glided along the woodpile. I heard a scratching noise. Lally was sharpening his claws. He said "Meow," and the night became friendly as he walked beside me, up the steps and into the kitchen.

Laurance waited in the glow of the lamp. "Well, fraidy-cat, nothing hurt you, did it?" he said.

"No." I handed him the egg. I sat at my place, hands in my lap, and fingered the sore place on my wrist where the hen had pecked me. A feeling of pride grew up within me. It was going to leave a scar.

Selling and Buying

THE FOLLOWING summer Mama had a new way to make a living. She had bought a surrey so she could drive the six miles to Sylvan Beach, a summer resort on Oneida lake, to sell home-made baked goods. In June we started out. Mama had baked two batches of bread—white and whole wheat—the night before. Since three AM she had been baking cookies and pies. She packed the bread in huge shortening tins and put the pies in wooden cases Laurance had made. Dozens of sugar and molasses cookies were packed in market baskets. The whole back of the surrey was full. The boys squeezed onto the front seat and I sat on Joe's lap.

"Sit still," Joe said as I wriggled on his bony knees.

Mama held the lines. When Tom went slow she said, "Wiggle the whip," and whoever could grab the whip first gave it a shake in its socket. Startled, Tom speeded his pace. "I never have to hit him," said Mama. "He takes the hint."

Tom held back the heavily loaded surrey down the steep hill beyond the railroad station, then trotted toward the Fish Creek Landing. The early morning was cool.

I hated to sell. Mama had fixed me a toy basket and made tiny five-cent pies for me to sell. In the basket were a half dozen each of sugar and molasses cookies. Over my wares she spread a snowy napkin. "You don't have to carry bread," she said. "But be sure to tell them about it."

Joe and Laurance didn't mind selling. When we came to the first cottages they leaped out with full-sized baskets and sprinted away.

"Go," said Mama. "You won't mind when you've done it a while."

Reluctantly I walked up the steps of the first house and knocked on the door. I hoped no one was home. A frowzy-haired woman in a bathrobe opened the door.

"Good morning, Madam," I recited. "Would you like to buy fresh home-made cookies, bread or pies?" While saying these words I lifted the corner of the napkin.

With a scowl she said, "No, thank you," and slammed the door.

At the next place a boy my age came to the door. I asked, "Is your mother home?" He ran into the back room. His mother, bigger than Mama, waddled out. "Good morning, Madam, would you like to buy—"

"Not interested," she said before I'd lifted the napkin. "I don't buy at the door." From behind her the boy made faces at me. My cheeks burned.

Mama drove to the next bunch of houses. She got down, hitched Tom to a tree, and lifted out her basket. "Come with me," she said. "Watch how I do." She marched resolutely up to a house and knocked sharply. A housewife opened the door. "Good morning, Madam," Mama beamed. "Would you like to buy fresh home-made cookies, bread or pies?" Before her spiel was finished she had drawn the napkin back to reveal neatly packed rows of cookies and a loaf each of white and whole wheat bread. The woman glowered, but Mama didn't give her a chance to speak. "I baked them myself," she said with enthusiasm. "They're made with pure vegetable shortening and the best flour. My pies have only fresh fruit picked on the farm. Would you like to see an apple, cherry or blueberry pie?"

"Fresh bread," the woman murmured. She poked the crust. "I wouldn't have to bake." She stared into the basket. "I'll take a loaf of this white bread, and maybe an apple pie. But I'd have to see it first."

Mama turned to me. "Run get an apple pie," she said. "Be careful, don't drop it."

I took one of Mama's thick, juicy, cinnamony pies from the case and walked back to the house.

"It does look good," said the housewife. "How much?"

"Ten cents for the bread. Thirty for the pie."

"Pretty dear," the woman said. "But, after all, this is my vacation. I'll take them."

As we went to the next house Mama said brightly, "See how easy? Let them get a good look and they'll be tempted. You'll catch on." I never did catch on, but now and then I sold a loaf of bread or a half dozen cookies, and two or three of the miniature pies—to mothers with children who begged for them.

When it was time to quit Mama hitched Tom to a tree near the beach. Oneida Lake, fifteen miles long and five miles wide, stretched before us, its water blended with the sky. On the creamy sand, whitecaps broke in long ruffly lines. "Get into your suits," said Mama. "You can swim for an hour." She held a blanket between us and the street while we changed.

"Last one in's a rotten egg," yelled Laurance as he raced to the water.

"I'll duck you," said Joe, on his heels. They threw themselves in with a splash, then lunged into the breakers. Clad in Laurance's old suit, I scampered to the water's edge and let a foamy wave lap my feet. As the wave ebbed I jumped back, afraid of the crawling sand under my soles. Mama spread a blanket on the sand and sank upon it. "Don't go too far!" she called to the boys. And to me, "Just wade at the edge when the boys aren't with you."

It wasn't long before Mama called, "Come here, children. It's time to go." We raced to get dressed. Mama gave us each a nickel for ice cream and we bought cones. "Why does your forehead ache when you eat ice cream?" I asked Mama.

"I don't know."

"It's to tell you you're a pig," said Laurance. "It only happens when you eat too fast."

"Your brains are in your forehead," said Joe. "It's freezing your brains."

Tom whinnied from the surrey, and pawed the dirt. When we gave him ice cream he got a funny look on his face and moved his head back and forth. Every little while he curled up his top lip and stretched out his muzzle, while foam dribbled from his tongue.

"Here's cookies left over," said Mama. "Divide with Tom."

We took a different road home. It passed by a watering trough. Tom turned to it, sank his nose deep and sent circles out to lap the mossy sides. My mind traced Tom's face with its white star reflected in the water, and the crystal drops on his velvet lips. I wanted to see better, and struggled in Joe's arms. "I want to get out," I said.

"No," said Mama. "Don't let her down, Joe. We're going right on."

"I want to see Tom drink," I insisted.

"Why, you see him all the time," said Mama. "Don't be foolish." She tightened the lines and said, "Come on, Tom." She slapped the lines but Tom didn't budge. He freed his head and plunged his muzzle up to his eyes. He dabbled, shook his head and sipped a few swallows.

"He's playing!" I squealed. "Look, Mama, he's playing in the water just like me."

Mama smiled. "He's playing, all right. But we've got to get on. That's enough, Tom." She pulled him firmly away.

Mama gave the boys each a quarter and me a dime. "Make sure you take out the tithe," she said. "God's tenth is not yours to spend."

We had bread and milk for supper, with huckleberry pie for dessert. "Can you eat half?" asked Mama, as she poised a sharp knife over a pie.

"Half'll do," said Laurance.

My spoon mashed the middle of the crust down into the sweet purple filling. When the pie was gone I ran my fingers round and round the bowl.

"Aren't you through?" asked Mama.

"I'm making pictures. See? There's waves like at the beach."

"Your fingers are messy," she said. "Stop it, and help clear the table."

I saved money for the one thing I wanted most. Joe had made himself a guitar out of a cigar box with rubber-band strings. It twanged like a real guitar. Sometimes he let me play it. I wanted a toy violin I had seen at the penny arcade. It cost a dollar. When I showed it to Mama she said, "Humph! It'll be broken in no time."

"But it really plays. Look how cute it is. It's in a red box."

"You're wasting your money."

Finally I brought it home. I put it under my chin and scraped the bow across the strings, expecting music. Instead, there was a scratchy sound.

"I told you so," said Mama.

"I don't care. I can use it to make believe." I took my fiddle to the porch and played for Lally, who purred and blinked his eyes as I scraped the strings and hummed.

In July wild huckleberries ripened. We went berrying in Watson's field four miles away. Along the narrow sandy road trees grew so close that we could snatch twigs as we rode past, and low branches slapped the buggy. Just before the field came Stoner's Hill. We all got out to walk up. Head down, Tom threw his weight against the breast-band and scrabbled upward. His feet loosened stones and made them roll down the hill. The boys kept ahead. I caught hold of the back of the buggy and let it pull me while my feet hopped in giant steps.

"Let go that buggy!" said Mama. "Tom's got enough to pull without you."

In Watson's field we grabbed pails and rushed to the

bushes. I fastened a two-quart pail on my belt. The boys used four-quart pails. Wild huckleberries grew scattered in a field overgrown with bracken, chokecherry and maple. We waded through patches of low-bush blueberries to bushes which towered over our heads. Some berries were big as our thumbnails.

My fingers curved over a bunch of blue, red and green berries, automatically sorted the ripe ones, and let them drop into the pail. Horseflies swarmed. I stamped my feet and flicked my shoulders like Tom to keep the flies away. While the boys went deeper in, Mama picked next to me. She went bareheaded, her dark hair, thick and wavy, making a shield from flies and sun. Sweat trickled from her damp hair and curls lay wet on her forehead.

The field throbbed with life. Towhees nested in grass clumps. The male with his striking black, tan and white markings, cried, "Chewink!" as I came near his nest. He scratched like a chicken in dry leaves under the bushes. He flew to a low chokecherry branch to cry, "*Drink* your tea!"

"I've found a towhee's nest," yelled Laurance. I ran to him and saw four white eggs sprinkled with brown dots like cinnamon. The nest was a cup of grass perfectly formed, blended into dry grass and leaves on the ground. Over it arched a frond of bracken.

"Probably a second brood," said Laurance.

The parent birds flitted from branch to branch, crying sharply. "Get away, children," called Mama. "Don't keep the bird from her nest."

Along the stone wall near me a chipmunk scurried, cheeks stuffed with berries. He ran tail straight up, froze to look and listen, then, like a rolled bead, he vanished into a crack. I saw another chipmunk crawl along a slender twig to reach ripe berries. At the end it dipped under his weight and turned him over. Upside down, he reached for the berries. When his cheeks were crammed, he swung upward and made his way back along the limb. Mourning doves cooed from a pine grove across the wall. Beyond ran a stream under leaning alders.

"Bet I can find a dove's nest," said Laurance. He walked along the wall. A bird flew from almost over his head on whickering wings. "I told you," said Laurance. He bent the branch so I could see in. Two white eggs lay on a flimsy platform of sticks. "Won't they fall out?" I asked.

"They could, but it's unlikely," said Laurance. "It's just the dove's way of raising her young."

We ate lunch in the shade next to Tom, with his oats and water pail, and shared our peanut-butter sandwiches with him.

The afternoon passed. As the sun got low Mama said, "We'd better go."

Tom's feet went clip-clop; wheels grated over stones; the buggy swayed. I fell asleep in Joe's lap. In the kitchen I roused up to eat a bowl of bread and milk, then dropped into bed, where visions of berries, chipmunks and birds whirled me to sleep.

The fall I was in third grade I took a jackknife to school. Joe and Laurance were expert whittlers. Joe had a huge knife with a stag handle and Laurance had a smooth-handled one. They'd got them with their own money.

When I'd saved thirty cents I bought one with a pearl handle which just fitted my hand. I carved horses from bits of wood and sandstone. Laurance carved cog wheels, trying to make an engine. Joe made willow whistles and darts.

I hit on a plan to be different. In Fox's *Book of Martyrs* were pictures of tortured saints. I was haunted by fear that torture would be too much for me to endure. Here was a way to prove how brave I was; I would cut a square of flesh out of my own hand. It would be a test of endurance.

Alone in my seat at school, I began my experiment. Each time the knife point was about to pierce my skin the nerves screamed, "Stop!" I couldn't do it. Again and again I steeled myself, but when the hurt came I backed away.

About this time, Rajamak came. He rode into the yard on a bicycle and Mama hired him to work in the woods. He was a stocky, red-faced Finn who spoke broken English. He had a yellow knife smaller than mine. After supper he sat in the living room with a piece of wood and carved reindeer and other animals. He decorated a board with carved heads of wheat for Mama to cut bread on. And for me he made a horse.

For three evenings he had been busy with a bit of pine board. I saw the shape of a horse emerge, with broad shoulders, a thin neck, and slender, perked-up ears. Rajamak stood the figure on the table beside my books. "For you," he said. As I reached for it he said, "Wait. I make something more." His rough hands fiddled with a scrap of wood, the small blade diving and paring, till he had fashioned a collar to fit over the horse's head. "Put it on," he said. "Harness your horse."

The toy was better than a doll. I carried it to school,

and at my desk put the collar on and off, while in my mind the wooden horse and I worked in the woods, plowed and cultivated crops and went on trips to town.

Rajamak left in spring, riding the bicycle on which he had come. We never saw him again. But I treasured the wooden horse and collar for years.

Sister Arnold

THE SUMMER I was eight, Sister Arnold came to stay with us. Mama needed help with her baking and Sister Arnold needed a home for herself and her foster children, John and Gladys. Sister Arnold and six-year-old John took one of the bedrooms. Gladys, who was my age, slept with me. She was pretty, with naturally curly hair. In the mornings she wailed, "Oh, my hair! It's so frizzy I can't comb it."

"I wish I had curly hair."

"It's horrid. When it's damp it won't lie down." She gave her hair a pat, withdrew her hand, and the hair sprang up in bright, lively curls. I gazed into the mirror as she set the curls into waves and saw a smirk of pride on her face.

I turned away.

With the Arnolds' coming everything changed. Sister Arnold was a tall, gangling woman with messy hair falling out of a low bun. She walked stooped as though weights were tied to her hands. She talked in a singsong voice. Goats were her hobby. She brought goats with her for wholesome milk, and from somewhere came bags of dates, boxes of special flour and brown rice. Sugar was taboo. We could no longer have it on our mush or in Postum, and she got Mama to cut down on cookies and pies. "Olive oil on the bread," she prescribed firmly. "It's more wholesome than margarine."

Mama took to all these changes. "Sister Arnold is an authority on health foods," she said. "She's brought a whole new way of life."

"A horrible way," said Joe.

"Taste doesn't matter. It's nutrition that counts," Laurance mocked Sister Arnold. "John's a good example. He looks as though he'll croak any minute."

John tagged along with us, peevish and fretful, wherever we went. Gladys mothered him while Sister Arnold worked in the kitchen or out with her goats. She had partitioned off the empty stall next to Tom, where a door let the goats come and go to pasture. Always before I could go into the pasture any time. If Tom were there he'd look up and come toward me to see if I had a handful of grass or a cookie. Then I'd walk along beside him as he grazed.

The nannies were hornless and gentle, but the buck chased me and butted. Not only did his horns hurt, but they knocked me down. He never attacked Sister Arnold.

Everything went wrong. The good horse smell of the barn was replaced by the stench of goats. The pasture was ruled by the buck. Our food was robbed of flavor. I had to put up with John's whining and fight my envy of

Gladys. In addition, Sister Arnold tried to boss me. But worse was to come.

Mama was a strict vegetarian, in the limited sense of eating no meat, fish nor fowl. She frowned on cheese and eggs. Joe's chickens produced eggs which she served us sparingly and used in baking, but she never killed a chicken for food.

At Grandma's I had seen dead chickens, on rare occasions when she served chicken and dumplings to guests. I had heard her say briskly, "I'll get Dar to kill me a chicken." If he wasn't around she'd kill the chicken herself. She carried the squawking bird by the legs, upside down, and chopped her head off with the ax.

To please Sister Arnold, Mama had agreed to take dressed fowl in the surrey for customers. Much as I hated to sell, there was joy in handling fluffy bread, crisp cookies and juicy pies. The aroma of baking permeated our kitchen and wafted from the back seat of the surrey. Now I was to see bloody ends of necks where heads had been; pimpled bodies; naked wings; and stiff yellow legs which would never again scratch for corn or race through the barnyard. As I crept about the house I tried not to smell the pails of hot water into which chickens were plunged before plucking, and gray masses of wet feathers lying in heaps. I avoided the sharp knives that had cut their bodies. In the surrey I stubbornly refused to handle the carcasses and shrank from them as far as possible.

The summer passed. John and Gladys went to school with us. Christmas came. Mama didn't believe in Christmas. "It's a pagan holiday," she said. "Not truly a celebration of Christ's birth." However, she let us have a tree and she knitted mittens and stockings to give us.

Papa sent tinsel and paper bells and books and ribbon candy. Aunts and uncles sent toys.

Strangely, Sister Arnold made a big thing of Christmas. She had Grandpa cut a huge tree and set it in a corner of the living room. She asked Mama to lock the door. In the mail came big and little boxes from New York City, where John's and Gladys' parents lived. Sister Arnold stored them in the living room, relocking the door after each addition. She and Mama spent Christmas Eve trimming the tree.

Christmas morning I got up before the other children, and I huddled in the hall outside the living room door. From the kitchen came sounds of Mama as she started the fire and pumped water for the teakettle. Joe and Laurance slid down the banister, shouting, "Merry Christmas!" Joe tried the door. "Still locked." He lay on the floor, his eye to the crack under the door.

At the top of the stairs Sister Arnold loomed, holding John by the hand. Gladys padded behind them. Mama joined us, the door was unlocked, and we all marched in. There was a tree such as I'd never seen. A silver star touched the ceiling. Ornaments sparkled and tinsel blazed from every bough. Boxes were piled under the tree, clear to the branches. Sister Arnold with her long bleak face acted as Santa Claus. Box followed box into the arms of Gladys and John. Gladys had two new dresses, toys galore and a beautiful doll. John opened toys and books, pajamas and games, fancy candy and a brand-new sled.

It was the doll I envied most. She had long blonde curls, a rose-colored dress and a cunning plush jacket with muff to match. Her arms and legs were jointed, her eyes opened and closed. She said "Mama" when you turned her over. Joe and Laurance each got a book from Papa, hand-knit socks and mittens from Mama and a few toys from relatives. I got similar gifts.

After breakfast we children went out to play. John's sled was a Flexible Flyer bigger than Joe's. At Baker's Hill Joe pulled John on the sled to the top. There he told John to get off. "I'm going to test it," he explained. He threw the rope back, clasped the long sled and ran forward. Slam! He took a bellywhacker and shot down the hill, weaving this way and that as he played with the steering gear.

John hopped about, wailing in his thin, cracked voice, "It's my sled!"

"Your brother's mean," said Gladys.

One day when Mama came back from town I ran to her as she put up Tom. "I don't want the Arnolds here," I said. "They spoil everything."

Mama lifted off the harness and hung it up. She took off the bridle and slipped the halter on.

"Mama, why does Sister Arnold have to stay here?" I said, as I ran my hand over Tom's thick winter coat.

"She's a help to me," said Mama. "You know Gladys' and John's parents are well off. She gives me some of what they pay her. The goats' milk saves us money, too. I don't know how I'd have gotten by this winter without her."

"Don't we help?" I asked.

"You do your chores, but you don't understand all there is to do. I need a grown woman's help." She pushed past me in the narrow stall. "You can get Tom's grain," she said. "Be sure to fasten the bin."

Tom whinnied when he heard the grain bin open. As I poured the oats into his feedbox I got a whiff of his warm, fragrant breath, which blotted out the rank odor of goat. Mama brought a forkful of hay. "I hate Sister Arnold and Gladys and John," I blurted out, while the blat of a goat came from the boarded-up stall next door.

"You mustn't say that. Love they neighbor. Think of those poor children away from their parents, and Sister Arnold trying to take care of them."

"They have everything. Look at Gladys' doll!"

"Your dolls are just as good as hers. What if they don't talk? You can talk to them and make believe." Fork in hand, Mama stood squarely in her galoshes, her worn coat bulging over her curves. "Now let's go in the house. And don't let me hear another word about hating. You pray to God to put love in your heart."

Glumly I followed her into the kitchen where Sister Arnold was setting the table. "I made a good rich soup of carrots and potatoes and turnips," she boasted the moment Mama came in. "I added a little olive oil, but no tomatoes. It's not good to mix acid vegetables with starch." I hated turnips and Mama knew it. Mama's soups had tomatoes and beans and wisps of dried parsley and she put margarine in. I washed and sat down to the table to glare at the watery soup with spots of pale oil floating on top.

Mama saw that I was mad so she picked me to say the blessing. "Thank you, God, for this food." I forced the words past stiff lips. "May it strengthen us to do Thy will. Amen."

With the coming of spring I had nightmares about the chickens. Sister Arnold placed triangular boxes all around the barnyard with setting hens cooped inside. As the chicks hatched, they could run through the slatted front while the hen clucked anxiously inside, unable to mother them unless they came to her. She paced back and forth behind the slats, and poked her head through. When any of us came near she ruffled her feathers, clucked and squawked in frenzy, calling her chicks to warn them of danger.

When the chicks had grown a little, Sister Arnold put them in a pen to fatten for market. I had never seen such a thing. On Grandpa's farm chickens of all ages lived together, and Joe's chickens lived that way too. They established their own social order, with the rooster as boss. The laying hens hopped into their nests when they felt like it and a mother hen herded her chicks into a corner and pecked the rooster if he came near.

These chickens were white, slender and uniform. "Excellent broilers," said Sister Arnold. "They'll be fat just as the beach season opens." So the white crowd who ate and sang like other chickens would have their heads cut off, their feathers scalded. I prayed that God would not let it happen. Mama said that God could tell if you really meant what you said, and I meant it. I also meant the hatred with which my heart was crammed.

When the Arnolds left it was like an answer to prayer. One day a man came in a wagon and took away all the white chickens. Another man loaded up the goats. Sister Arnold began to pack. The next day Mama took her and Gladys and John to the train.

"God works in mysterious ways," said Mama at supper. "Sister Arnold had to leave, but I've got someone else to help me this summer. Cousin Grace is coming."

She arrived two days after the close of school in late May. She was a strict school teacher with a tolerant smile. When children made a mistake, she said, "They're only young'uns." One by one she hugged us to her, not minding when our arms skewed her hat around. Her coat was baggy like Sister Arnold's but she was not slovenly. I rushed to bring out my treasures, and in her upstairs room she let me show them as she hung up her hat and coat and put things in bureau drawers. "Here's something for you," she said. It was a small golden slipper, stuffed and covered with red velvet to make a pincushion. "That was my mother's," said Cousin Grace. "I thought you might like it."

I ran and hugged her. In my room I put the slipper on my bureau, where it saw itself in the glass.

Cousin Grace cleaned the house, washed the dishes, made a garden. She cooked meals and helped Mama bake. We children sold baked goods. Mama had time to take on more papering jobs and piano lessons.

That summer I bought a photograph album with letters burned into the leather cover.

Love and Need

SEPTEMBER came and I entered the fourth grade. That was the year I covered all my books with flour-sack jackets, decorated with pictures of animals and flowers. I developed a signature, a crude HS with winding tendrils, almost like Papa's twiggy EJS that adorned every one of his pictures.

From clippings and pictures he sent I learned that he was a well-known artist who wrote and illustrated articles about nature. He painted twelve of the Audubon Leaflets, which featured full-color bird paintings teamed with outline drawings on good paper for children to color.

Papa sent me copies of poems he had written, illustrated with sketches of birds. My favorite was "To a Lark."

> Far more than sky, with sun or starry train,
> Green fields or barren brown to him are worth;
> He seeks no closer view of Heaven to gain;
> He soars but for a better view of Earth.

The day before Christmas Papa knocked on the door, just as we were finished with breakfast. Mama let him in. The boys gathered up their books and found their mittens, ready for school. I wasn't going that day because I had a cold. Mama watched Papa stamp snow from his boots. "How are you?" He tossed the question into the smoky air of the kitchen, addressed to me.

"All right," I mumbled. I swished oatmeal around in my dish. I couldn't talk to Papa with Mama there.

"When does school let out?" he asked the boys.

"Four o'clock."

"I'll be here," he said.

"We're late," said Laurance. He and Joe dashed out the door.

There was a moment of silence; then Mama said stiffly, "Won't you sit down? I'll get you a cup of Postum."

As he took a chair, Papa's quick eyes darted around the room. Mine followed his, to the torn shades still drawn against the night; wallpaper stained by a leak in the roof; the cracked glass of the door and the worn linoleum, where a puddle of water spread from the melting snow of his boots. As Mama set a chipped cup before him he said: "All the comforts of home!"

A flush rose in Mama's cheeks. She spooned Postum into his cup and poured hot water. Papa selected a spoon from the holder, examined it, wiped it with his napkin. He dumped three heaping teaspoons of sugar into his Postum and stirred. With his other hand he flicked crumbs, like bugs, from the oilcloth.

I saw everything Papa saw, and more. I saw the spread table, the warm kitchen fire, the cleanness of the floor besmirched by his wet boots. I wanted to send him away.

Instead I meekly stirred my oatmeal, eyes on my plate. I wanted something from Papa. After breakfast we went to the living room while Mama stayed in the kitchen.

"Are you going to have a tree this year?" he asked.

"No."

"I was afraid so," he said. "I brought something for you, though. You'll know what it is tomorrow. Now, what would you like me to draw?"

"A horse!"

I watched him bring out paper and pencil from the knapsack beside him. Screwing up courage I decided to ask again for what I wanted most. "Papa, couldn't you buy me a horse? One all my own, so I could ride?"

"If you were with me, you'd have the most beautiful horse in the world," he said. "He'd be all yours, just for your pleasure." He sketched an airy creature with flowing mane.

My heart surged. While his hands were busy his face changed and his voice became bitter. "I can't give you one," he said. "I won't buy a horse for your mother to work to death. I'd want you to have a saddle horse. Your mother'd put him to the plow."

"That wouldn't matter. I'd let him work, but I could ride him. Tom works too much, and he's not mine. Please, Papa, I want a horse of my own."

"How would you feed him? If I sent money it'd go to the church. The horse wouldn't get it, and neither would you."

"He'd work and pay for his feed. I'd take care of him. I'd love him."

"I'm sorry," he said. He reached out his hand, but I flung it away.

"You don't love me," I said.

"I wish I didn't love you so much." He rose from his chair, letting the sketch drop to the floor, and left the house.

Christmas morning he came and talked to Mama a long time behind a closed door. Then he took over the living room. When he called us in we found that he had draped a straight chair with tinsel and hung red paper bells on the back. On the seat lay a heap of presents, among them a cotton Santa Claus with a red sleigh full of candy, and for me a pad of drawing paper and a set of watercolors.

The next day he was gone. "I'm going back West," he said. "I'm not wanted here." His voice was cold, his eyes remote.

Scribbled notes arrived from Michigan, Nebraska, Montana. He sent me a bag of salt from Utah and a grizzly bear carved of wood from Yellowstone Park. That Christmas the package he sent me was thin. I opened it to find a framed copy of the song, "My Rosary," by Robert Cameron Rogers, hand-lettered and illustrated with watercolor scenes. A young girl laughed under an apple tree, her hands full of bloom. A tall man stood silhouetted at sunset against western hills. When I showed the poem to Mama she said, "Yes, it's nice," before she turned away. Dimly I felt the meaning of "The hours I spent with thee," and the "barren gain and bitter loss," but the paintings were more real than the words. I hung the poem so I could see it from my bed.

Mama too had received a gift from Papa. She opened it in secret. The following morning I saw a new frame on the living-room wall. It held a poem with pictures of a small home nestled among trees, smoke curling up, lamplight streaming from cozy windows at dusk. The poem said

Where there is love, there is God,
And where there is God, there is no need.

It hung there like a puzzle. Papa didn't believe in God. And if he and Mama loved each other, why weren't they together?

Spring came. A May breeze stirred the dimity curtains and brought the fragrance of lilacs into the kitchen. While the breakfast oatmeal simmered, Mama stepped out the back door and broke sprays of lilacs from the row of gnarled bushes north of the house. She reached up to the tallest bush and added one sprig of snow-white bloom to the armful of purple. At the table she arranged them in a brown crock. "When lilacs last in the dooryard bloomed," she murmured. Her fingers played among the flowers. "Your father—"

"What about Papa?"

"The white lilac was his favorite. Once when you were a baby he brought me a whole bunch from the florist. And no milk in the icebox for your supper!" She shoved the crock to the center of the table. "I'll dish your oatmeal," she said and bustled to the stove.

"But, Mama—"

"Pshaw! Eat your oatmeal, or you'll be late for school."

As I finished my oatmeal, hooves sounded in the driveway. Grandpa's voice called, "Whoa!" Perched high on the seat of the lumber wagon, he held Big Tom and Baron in, their ponderous barrels and muscled haunches dwarfing his wiry frame. His grizzled mustache hid most of his face, over which a battered hat was pulled low. From beneath the brim glittered his steel-framed glasses. "Good Morning, May. Good Morning, Hope. I'm harrowing the west field for early potatoes. Call me when it's sharp noon."

While Grandpa talked I was at the horses' heads, petting their muzzles. Grandpa's fists jerked the lines. "Get away from there, child." He told Mama, "It'll take me two days to get those potatoes in, then I'll get at your roof that's leaking." He slapped the lines.

I scurried out the yard and off to school.

I came home in time to see Grandpa drive away. The next day after school I hurried to the field where he planted potatoes in the newly harrowed field. "Start dropping," he called from the middle of a row. "I'll go back and cover up." He handed me a pail of sprouting potato pieces. "Put two to a hill."

I let my bare feet sink into crumbly earth and dropped two chunks at a time. The sun shone warm. A breeze blew from the south bringing wave after wave of apple blossom scent. From the distant orchard drifted a robin's hymn to the coming rain. Before dusk the planting was finished. Grandpa and Mama went out back of the house and looked at the lilacs.

"Those bushes shade the roof," said Grandpa. "They'll have to go."

"No, Papa." Mama's voice was mild.

"They're rotting the house," said Grandpa.

"You can fix the house. But I want those lilacs left right where they are."

"Dang it all," yelled Grandpa. His eyes glared. His mustache quivered. "The house'll fall down on you. I'm going to pull them out."

"Please!" said Mama. Grandpa didn't answer. He hitched up his team and rumbled out the driveway.

The next day Mama had me stay home from school to fetch tools for Grandpa, while he fixed the roof. When he arrived she was already in the buggy. "I'm going to McConnellsville," she said. "Hope'll wait on you." She turned to me. "I won't be back at noon. You warm up food for Grandpa." Tom trotted off for McConnellsville. Grandpa drove to the barn. Later I heard the stamp of horses' feet, and Grandpa's voice cried, "Haw, there!" He had driven back of the house. I rushed to look out the screen door. The horses, hitched to a chain, had backed close to the lilacs.

Aghast, but helpless, I saw the heavy chain linked around the base of a bush, heard Grandpa speak to the horses, and watched the broken roots spring out of the ground. The fallen purple lilacs were dragged away, dirt dripping from their roots like blood from a wound. He left them in a heap and stalked back, the chain writhing and snapping through crushed weeds. My eyes blurred, my heart pounded. I looked at Mama's bouquet on the table, the sprig of white lilac like a flag. I went out to face Grandpa.

He had the chain around the white lilac. Stooping, he slipped the hook into a link and straightened up.

"Grandpa!" I cried. "Not that one."

He looked up, his face barbed by his mustache, eyes fortified behind their steel rims. "You too?" he said. "The egg telling the rooster how." He glanced upward to figure which way the bush would fall. "Get out of the way," he said.

"But, Grandpa—"

"Out of the way, child!"

I stepped back.

Grandpa shouted, "Giddup!" The traces tightened. The stately lilac toppled, slow like in a nightmare. As the horses pulled, it slithered along the ground, nodding its white head as if to say goodbye.

I went back to play, but my doll's faces accused me. When I tried to read I could barely see. After a while I heard Grandpa call and I went out. Beside the kitchen ell loomed a vast emptiness, where the rain-coming sky pressed too close. Above the rotted eaves, ragged shingles showed scars made by scratching limbs. "See!" said Grandpa. "The house was ready to go. Now fetch the hammer and nails from the woodshed." He drove off to the barn, singing, "When the Roll Is Called Up Yonder, I'll Be There," at the top of his voice.

In silence I handed Grandpa tools as he worked on the roof. At noon I served him food. By mid-afternoon the roof was finished, just before gray skies let go rain. As he drove off huddled against the downpour, I sat in the kitchen. Things were tight and snug now. The kitchen looked lighter with the shuttering bushes removed. My eyes strayed to where the fallen bushes lay, rain beating them into the ground. What would Mama say?

Tom's clop-clop sounded in the muddy driveway. When Mama struggled in with her burden of groceries I ran to help her. She put Tom away, then came back in.

"The roof's fixed," I said.

She moved to the north window. "I knew it," she said. "I knew he'd do it." Her hands crushed her wet skirt. "Let's get supper on," she said. "Go down cellar and get the potatoes and beans."

When I came up from the cellar Mama was bent over

the table, her face buried deep in the flowers. With a sigh she lifted brimming eyes to mine. She straightened her shoulders and turned to the stove.

Rain swept past the window. Mama lighted the lamp and set it on the table, where it cast a mellow glow as we sat down to eat. An old question bothered me, "Mama, why doesn't Papa live with us? Don't you love him anymore?"

"Yes, I love him," she said fiercely. "And he says he still loves me. 'Where there is Love . . . there is no need.' " She looked toward the window. "But we have to have a roof over our heads."

We ate in the yellow glow of the light, the bunch of flowers a separation between us. I longed to paint Mama's face in the lamplight; the flowers in the brown crock. If I could only paint the picture maybe I'd learn to understand.

At Aunt Emma's

After Christmas Mama took us children by train to my great aunt Emma's, where we were to stay for several months. Mama had a job cooking for a hospital in Middletown and couldn't have us with her. Grandpa took Tom and the cats and chickens down to his place to keep for us.

Aunt Emma's was our second home. She and Aunt Clara met us at the door with open arms. Aunt Clara bustled to the pantry and brought out leftovers, and plates heaped with cookies and doughnuts. She set out a pitcher of milk and cut an apple pie.

Aunt Emma and Mama discussed the Lawrence tribe. Aunt Emma's father was old Horace Lawrence, a farmer and an elder in the church. He used to go preaching in different towns, accompanied by his wife, and at the Old Homestead they had entertained visiting preachers and their wives. Emma, his spinster schoolteacher daughter, carried on the Lawrence tradition of hospitality. She had inherited the Old Homestead and it was still headquarters for the local church. Sabbath school was held in the kitchen and sermons preached in the living room. Aunt Emma had retired early and kept open house for countless nephews and nieces, including us.

We children ran outdoors. The big orchard out back was bare now. Snow lay drifted deep. The little brook in the pasture below was icebound. We went to the barn, where Aunt Emma's driving horse, Nellie, munched her hay. She was slow and fat, and a muddy brown color. Uncle Fred warned us to leave her alone. Uncle Fred had met and married Aunt Clara in Mooers Forks years before. They had a son who had died in infancy and another who was away studying to be a minister. Uncle Fred's bald head jerked nervously as he jabbed with his fork, cleaning Nellie's stable. His blue eyes, enlarged by thick lenses, bulged out like marbles. He was a small man with strong muscles and a harried manner. Uncle Fred always looked angry.

The Old Homestead was a rambling house stretched along Bangor Road, with a living room, kitchen and woodshed all in line. Across the back ran a screened porch which overlooked the orchard. Upstairs, the hallway divided the house squarely in two lengthwise, with doors opening to rooms on each side. Mine was a cubbyhole at the northwest end.

That night I creaked up the stairs behind Aunt Emma. She tucked me in snugly, gave me a kiss and said, "I'm glad you're here!" Her feet moved swiftly over the carpet and her form receded down the long hallway, silhouetted against the lamp in her hand.

The next morning Uncle Fred hitched up Nellie and

took Mama to the train in Brushton so she could travel to her new job.

We went to public school that year. I was in the fifth grade. For the first time I saw Compton's *Pictured Encyclopedia* and I spent every spare moment reading fairy tales and looking at pictures and copying them. That year long division was my biggest problem, but Aunt Emma tutored me at home. My room was next to hers and at bedtime I lay on her bed while she told me stories about her days of school teaching.

"I started teaching when I was sixteen," she began. "My first school was at Brandon. I didn't know the first thing about pedagogy. I remember that first terrible day. With fear and trembling, yet determined to succeed, I left home on a bright spring day. My brother Warren, who had driven me there, went away and I stood before a little schoolhouse, not knowing what awaited me inside.

"A dozen eager faces greeted me as I stepped in the door. I didn't know what to do, except what I had seen my own teachers do. I took the names of the pupils and assigned lessons. Every child had a different textbook.

"Fortunately it turned out to be an easy school. I loved the children. The schoolhouse was situated on the border of the vast forests of the Adirondacks. The woods were not far away, and in small groves near the schoolhouse we ate our dinner. I told the children stories of the early settlers and we would play it all out at noon. We had a 'Plymouth Rock' and went exploring. We made things so real that sometimes the little ones would cling to me in terror, expecting to see an Indian lurking behind a tree.

"I had never seen so many evergreens and May flowers as we found there. We decorated the schoolroom with them, and the children drew beautiful pictures. I had just begun the study of botany, and I found the flowers especially interesting.

"I received wages of three dollars a week, and had to pay room and board out of that. My brothers, Warren and Asa, came for me Friday afternoon so I could spend Sabbath and Sunday at home. Every weekday morning I walked two miles from my boarding place to school, and back in the afternoon, but I didn't mind."

Aunt Emma paused, her eyes far away. I snuggled deeper in bed. "Tell me about the Burke school," I prompted.

"The school at Burke was the best of all in my career as a teacher. I had taught at hard schools where children were backward or mean and quarrelsome and some where the surroundings were drab. Entering the Burke schoolroom you could feel love and friendship. It looked as though it was the very place described by Whittier: the warping floor, the battered seats, the jackknives' carved initial and even the charcoal frescoes on the walls and the door's worn sill—where, I was to find, cold wind blew in unmercifully on winter days.

"Most of the Burke children were under eight years of age, just beginning their school life. I joined in their games, held them when they got hurt, comforted them in trouble, told them stories—the same ones I've told you so many times.

"There was fat, rosy-cheeked Josie, Daisy with dark eyes and curls, little Floyd who cried half the first day, but later insisted on coming even when his parents wanted to keep him home, telling them that the teacher couldn't get along without him. There was Ruth, full of mischief, sober Paul and little Maude, who asked every afternoon, 'Have I been a good girl today?' Ruth, who never sat still a minute, used to wiggle around until she'd fall off the high, straight-backed seat."

Aunt Emma told me classics, including *Androcles and the Lion.* One story I liked best of all because it was about a horse was "The Story of the Bell." Years ago, in Italy, it went, there was a village which had an ingenious idea for helping people. In the middle of the village was a big bell, and attached to it was a rope hanging to the ground. When anyone was in trouble he could ring the bell and the leaders of the village would come and help him.

Near that village lived a horse who had a cruel master. The man beat him and made him work too hard, and also didn't give him enough to eat. The horse was starving. One day he ran away. He came to the village. It happened that the bell rope had broken and someone had tied a piece of grapevine on the end to lengthen it. The horse saw the grapevine, which still had green leaves on. As he reached up to eat the leaves, he made the bell ring.

The village leaders hurried to find out who was in trouble. They found the thin, hungry horse. "Who will give this horse a home and plenty to eat?" they asked. One man who needed a horse promised to take good care of him, and so he found a home.

At Aunt Emma's it was easy to be good. Like Grandma, she wanted us to behave, but when we failed it was not a life-and-death matter. We tried to do right to please her, not to escape hell fire.

Aunt Emma encouraged my artwork. Every day, from her desk she allowed me two sheets of unlined white paper on which to draw. She let me rummage in old trunks in the attic where she had stored pictures used in her teaching. I traced or copied the ones I liked best, and she pinned my work up in her room.

Each evening I went with Uncle Fred to the barn. A dour man, he seldom spoke to children, but he allowed me to watch him take care of Nellie if I kept out of his way. At chore time he lighted a lantern and hung it on a nail, where its glow cast shadows like giant ink blots. The stable was warm on winter nights, and as Nellie tossed her head and Uncle Fred wielded his fork, the shadows shifted.

I had made myself a barn, patterned after Nellie's stable and Grandpa's cow barn. One morning I sat on my bed and looked at my miniature barn, made from a cardboard box in which I had cut windows and doors. The doors swung out and in. The whole top was open so you could look in and see the stanchions for the cows; the tiny stalls and mangers for horses; and even a tack room with harness made of scraps of ribbon and jewelry Aunt Emma had given me.

The barn was mounted on a sheet of cardboard three feet square. The part extending beyond the box was colored to look like grass. On it stood cardboard horses and cows colored with crayon.

I had made a paper lantern for my stable. I knew a better lantern, however, but it wasn't mine. I wanted it just the same. A fight went on inside me as I sat on my bed beside my cardboard barn.

"It's not yours!"

"But I need it."

"Then ask Aunt Emma."

"She'd say no."

"You wouldn't want someone to take your things."

"But she never uses it. She wouldn't even know it was gone."

At the head of the stairs straight down the hall stood Aunt Emma's curio cabinet full of strange objects. Sometimes she would take time to open the glass door and bring her treasures out one by one, with a story about each. I went there now, and on the top shelf, between a chunk of petrified wood and two heathen idols, shone the one thing I wanted. It was a chinese lantern. Aunt Emma knew it from her botany study and told me it was the seed pod of the plant *Physalis francheti.* It was hollow, about an inch tall, and almost round. Although it was dry there was still a tinge of green in the stem. The globe itself was bright orange-red. It was like a lighted lantern; it would be perfect for my barn.

From the driveway came the clop of hooves. I ran to look out the window. There came Uncle Fred driving Nellie up from the barn. I heard Aunt Emma say goodbye to Aunt Clara and then the front door open and close. Craning my neck I watched Aunt Emma climb into the buggy. It was Friday and she was off to town. She would not be back until afternoon. Aunt Clara would be baking. Uncle Fred would be outdoors.

As soon as Nellie's footsteps faded I reached out and turned the knob of the cabinet. My throat had turned dry and my face burned. Once the door was open it was easy to pick up the lantern and feel its lightness. Aunt Emma would never miss it.

Gently I shut the door. As I turned to go, hasty footsteps sounded from the foot of the stairs and Laurance bounded up two steps at a time. My fist closed over the lantern and I hid my hand in the fold of my skirt.

"What're you up to?" Laurance asked.

"Nothing."

"You've been looking in Aunt Emma's cabinet."

"Y-yes."

Laurance's blue eyes took me in. "What's that in your hand?"

"N-nothing." He had come so suddenly that I couldn't think. My heart pounded and there was a blur before my eyes.

His arm lunged out and his strong hand gripped my shoulder. "Open up!" he demanded.

Reluctantly I opened my hand.

"What's that for?" he asked.

"It's a lantern—for my barn," I said miserably.

"What barn?"

I hadn't wanted to show him for fear he'd make fun. But he seemed interested. "Want to see it?" I asked.

"Sure."

Proudly I led the way to my room. When Laurance saw my creation he guffawed. "Call that a barn?" he said, as he hugged himself with his long arms. His brown hair, damp with sweat, lopped over his forehead as he laughed. He put out his hand and contemptuously tweaked one of the barn doors. "Not even hinges," he said.

"They fold out and in."

"Yeah. No glass in the windows, though. Where you going to put your lantern?"

"In here." I sat on the bed and reached into the stable and took out the crude paper lantern. With a piece of thread tied round the stem of *Physalis francheti* I hung my lantern on the paper-fastener nail. In the shaded interior of the barn the seed pod glowed.

"What will Aunt Emma say?" Laurance asked.

"You won't tell her, will you?"

"I'm no tattletale. But *you* know you took it. That's stealing."

"I'm just borrowing it," I told him. "I'll put it back when I'm through."

"You're crazy," said Laurance. "What do you want that old thing for, anyway?" He stuck out his finger and poked the fragile pod. it collapsed into dusty orange flakes, leaving the green stem trembling from its nail. "See? It's no good," he said. He ran out of the room.

My pulse thudded. Tears welled. How could I face Aunt Emma now? I gouged both fists into my eyes. I padded down the hall to the curio cabinet, my mind trying to put the lantern back. I peered in to the empty place—a small dark circle where the jaunty relic had kept dust from falling ever since I could remember. My legs grew weak. Tears again filled my eyes, but I brushed them away. Crying wouldn't help.

During supper Laurance didn't say a word, but when his eyes met mine they slid away. When we'd finished eating Aunt Emma and Aunt Clara cleared the table and did the dishes. I went to the living room and got a book. Uncle Fred was already in his armchair, but he never paid any attention to me. Soon Aunt Emma came in and sat down to read. I wanted to say something to her, but Uncle Fred was there. Then Aunt Clara joined us.

At bedtime I went silently upstairs and hid the barn under my bed. I had crept inside the covers when Aunt Emma came to say goodnight. "Did you say your prayers?" she asked, as she tucked me in. Yes, I had told God I was sorry. That was easy, because I couldn't see Him. But Aunt Emma was right in front of me, loving and trusting. I couldn't bear to see her face change. As she leaned over to kiss me I put my arms around her neck and hugged hard. I couldn't tell her. She patted the covers, took up the light and walked softly from the room, through the hall past the curio cabinet, on downstairs.

I began to make plans. I'd call and ask for a drink, I thought, then I'd tell her. Or when she came to bed I'd run to her room and snuggle and tell her in the dark. Amid these plans I fell asleep.

Next morning I jumped up early and brought my barn out from under the bed. I had hoped for a miracle. But there was the orange dust instead of the lantern. I heard footsteps and hastily shoved the box under the bed. Someone knocked. "Come in," I called.

Laurance strode through the doorway. "Did you tell her yet?" he asked.

"No."

"You'd better."

"I haven't had a chance," I said. A feeling hard and stubborn rose. I didn't need him to preach! "I was just going down to tell her," I said firmly. "Now get out of my room."

"We'll see," he muttered, as he backed out the door.

With slow steps I went downstairs. On the back porch Aunt Emma had started the washing. "What is it, dear?" she asked, sorting clothes. She had my red dress and one of Laurance's blue shirts in her hands. Before she could drop them on the pile I rushed to her, threw my arms around her neck and whimpered, "I'm sorry, Aunt Emma. I'm sorry."

She took me in her arms and listened as I confessed. "That's all right, dear," she soothed. "Now hush. Crying won't bring back the little lantern." She smoothed my hair. "But I know just how you can put everything right—and even better than before."

I looked up. She smiled mysteriously. "Would you spend your week's allowance to make things right?"

"Yes."

The following Friday she took me shopping with her, and at the feedstore asked me to spend my dime on a package of chinese-lantern seed. "For a long time I've been wanting to raise some," she said. "But I never got around to it. You'll be doing me a favor."

When spring came I planted the seeds in rows, and the rest of the summer weeded and hoed while the plants grew slowly. I was disappointed that they would not bear seeds until the coming year. Aunt Emma promised to pick the best one to put in her curio cabinet and save several choice ones for me.

Spruce Gum

THE SUMMER I was ten Joe went West to be with Papa. Laurance and I stayed on at Aunt Emma's. There were so many exciting things to do that Laurance decided not to work after all. His first project was to make a saddle for Tom. We didn't know anyone who rode in a saddle, but we wanted to be real cowboys.

"I know I can do it," he said, as he studied pictures in the Sears catalog. "Look at this one. Thirty dollars. Costs as much as a horse. The cheapest one's this army saddle for $4.50. See, it's got wood inside, with leather fastened over. I can make one almost like it for nothing." He slapped the catalog shut and together we raced to the barn.

Laurance rummaged in corners and fiddled with bits of old harness straps, rusty rings and broken halters. "We can use some of these for stirrup straps," he said. "The hard part will be the frame."

Every day we hoed several rows in Aunt Emma's

garden. Laurance had to fill the woodbox and I had to make beds and wipe dishes. But every spare moment we spent on the saddle. I held wood while Laurance shaped two pieces roughly, first with the ax and then with a jackknife. He nailed them together at the peaked front and wired them at the back. He bored holes by burning with heated wire. Aunt Emma let him use the fire in the cookstove.

He lugged the clumsy rig to the pasture, tried it on Tom, and carved and shaped until the wood fitted snugly over Tom's spine. "Now for the stirrup straps," he said. "We'll put them on and figure out stirrups later." He spliced broken straps, hammered in copper rivets, and put the extended strap over the wooden shape perched on a sawhorse so the ends of the strap would hang down.

"All we need is padding," he said. In the grain room he flapped the dust out of feed bags and filled them with hay. We took the stuffed bags to the sawhorse, where he molded the padding to fit the framework, the horse, and the rider. At last it was done, all sewed together with strong carpet thread donated by Aunt Clara. The girth was made of canvas sewn to straps.

For stirrups Laurance tried bending green sticks, but they broke. He formed loops in straps but they pinched our feet. Before he'd solved this problem Aunt Emma settled it by forbidding the use of stirrups at all. "They're dangerous," she said. "Men have been dragged by a foot and killed."

Laurance abandoned the idea of fixed stirrups, but he made a loop in each end of a rope and threw the rope across the saddle. It would fall if a rider was thrown. We'd still have to find a wall or a high place from which to mount, but while in the saddle our feet could rest. Laurance eased Tom up to a big rock, jumped into the saddle and thrust his sneaks into the stiff rope loops. Off he went on a trial run, headed toward South Bangor, where an old iron-kettle watering trough made a worthwhile goal.

After a while he came back, jouncing in the saddle, the looped rope slung across Tom's withers. He jumped down and started to undo the cinch.

"Don't I get a turn?"

"It's no good," he said as he worked a buckle loose. "When I started to post, one foot went down, the other went up, and I fell off."

"What did Tom do?"

"I yelled whoa and he stopped. I led him the rest of the way and got back on from the rim of the trough. Riding bareback's better than this clumsy thing." He carried the stirrupless saddle to the loft and buried it in the hay. Then he asked Aunt Emma for boards to start his next project—a boat that would stay afloat. I helped him saw, nail and caulk. We painted the boat green and carried it down the half mile to Big Brook, where we rowed back and forth on Sucker Pond with oars made of boards. It hardly leaked at all.

One morning in June, Cousin Percy came down to Aunt Emma's. He was driving Mabe, a rangy bay mare with black points, who had ears so long they made her look like a mule. He took Laurance and me back with him for a visit to his farm, Spruce Crest Hill, seven miles away. Mabe trotted fast along the level, up the rolling hills and down the other side. Though afflicted with heaves she had the long legs and willing heart of a good buggy horse. At the last hill, which rose steep and crooked to the house perched high above, Laurance and I jumped out and climbed on foot. We had plans for the day. “Let’s get to the pasture,” said Laurance. “I know where you can dig out spruce gum by the barrel. Great big chunks.”

“May I have your knife some of the time?” I asked.

“No, I’ll need it myself. Didn’t you bring yours?”

“Mine’s lost.”

“Too bad for you.”

We came into the yard, and there Cousin Loraine met us. She stood in sunlight, smoothing her house dress and fussing with her hair. She looked lovely in a frail, drooping way, her pale-brown hair swirled high like a peaked mushroom on a tall stem. “Hello, Laurance,” she called. “And Hope. So glad you came up today.” She pulled me to her. “My, you’ve grown. Like a weed.” She held me close for a moment, tousling my hair with her slender fingers. She let me go, saying, “Run and play now. I know you want to get to the woods.”

Cousin Loraine didn’t have any children. Couldn’t have—she let everyone know. She was delicate. Our elders had warned us not to stay to meals, for she complained about the work. She’d sigh and say, “I love to have them. Oh, if only I were stronger.” She always urged us to stay, however, and we stayed.

Spruces grew thick along the edge of the sugarbush, and the air was redolent with their balm. Laurance led me on as he restlessly darted from tree to tree, in search of good gum. These were all young ones with no accumulation of pitch. “Farther on,” he said. “Down by the creek.”

My bare feet padded along the winding path made by cows going down to drink. In one place grew a dense clump of hemlocks where the cows had made many paths as they brushed off flies under the bristly, low-sweeping boughs. I loitered there, my feet caressed by cool earth. A screech from Laurance sent me onward. When I got to the creek he was already up a spruce tree, hacking at a scarred crotch with his knife. He dug out a big hunk of resin and put it into his mouth. "Yum. Yum." he said, making believe the gum wasn't bitter. I knew it was bitter, but I wanted some. "It's all too high up," I said.

"All right. Here, I'll get you some." He shinned farther up the spruce, which leaned over the water. A carpet of needles scratched the bottoms of my feet. I watched a mud-dauber wasp gather mud at a wallow punched full of holes by cows' hooves while on my face I felt the sun distilling the essence of spruce. "Here, catch!" yelled Laurance. A dark brown, sticky blob fell into my out-stretched palms. Along one edge lay a feathery amber crust.

Laurance slid down. "Come on, sissy, chew it." His own jaws worked smoothly. "You've got to chew the bitterness out."

I put the gum in my mouth. Then I spit it right back in my hand. "I don't want it. It's horrid.

"I told you it was bitter. But the bitterness doesn't last. Put it in your mouth, now, and chew it—or *I'll never bring you with me again.*" The bitter juice almost choked me, but I kept on. After a while the gum had become smooth and elastic and the bitter taste was gone.

In the pasture we climbed lichened boulders big as houses. We teetered along the top of a stone wall and came to the abandoned farmhouse which marked an adjoining farm, now part of Spruce Crest Hill. Under the roof blue daubers made their tunnels. They flew in heavily laden with mud. A phoebe flashed from under the eaves and we saw she had a nest. Laurance reached to feel four eggs, while the mother bird called harshly, flicking her tail from the branch of a maple. The ancient house with empty windows and caved-in roof was surrounded by hoof marks of cattle, where they came to stamp in the shade.

"We'll get the cows tonight," said Laurance. "I'll ride Boob and you can ride old Mabe." Boob was a coal-black five-year-old filly. She was headstrong, and Cousin Percy wouldn't let me ride her. Anyone could ride Mabe.

We explored the sugarbush and followed the stream, hopping from one mossy rock to another in its deep-shaded bed. I kept the cud of gum in my mouth, but spit out saliva instead of swallowing. When the sun showed noon we raced into the yard. Cousin Loraine had a basin and soap on the bench outside the back door. "Wash up for dinner, children," she said. "Percy's already sat down."

In the kitchen we found Cousin Percy at the head of the table, with places set for us at the sides. Cousin Loraine had picked a single red rose for the table.

"It's lovely," I said.

"Yes." She sighed. "Wish I had a decent vase to put it in."

Cousin Percy asked the grace and said, "Make out a meal, kids. There's plenty."

"I can't cook like I used to," said Cousin Loraine. "I'm so weak all the time. But you're welcome to what's here."

It was just her way. The food was delicious—mashed potatoes with real cream whipped in; small tender leaves of lettuce just picked; two eggs apiece fried in deep butter; fresh crispy cookies she must have made while we were in the woods. And all the rich cool milk we could drink.

Finished, Laurance and I slipped our spruce gum back in our mouths. We thanked Cousin Loraine for the meal. She gave a slight smile and held her hand to her forehead. "You're welcome, children. Oh, if only I could get out to the woods like you can. I'd love to pick the wild flowers, see the birds."

"Here, have some of my spruce gum," I offered. I took out my wad and broke it in two.

"No, thank you, dear." She motioned it away. "Things like that make me sick." I popped the gum back in my mouth, with all its bitterness melted away.

We hurried from the woods before milking time, climbed the stone wall, and there was Cousin Percy, cultivating corn with Mabe. He stopped at the end of the row. "I'll quit now," he said, as he bent to unhook the traces. He knotted them out of the way and with a big swing lifted me up square in the middle of Mabe's back. "You kids can ride the horses after the cows."

Soon Laurance and I were mounted bareback on Boob and Mabe. The cows roamed sixty acres among patches of pasture and wooded swamp. We dug our heels into the horses' sides and trotted forward. As we skirted clumps of wild blackberries, reined our mounts around rocks, we listened for the lead cow's bell. We topped a rise, alert for bears (a black bear had been seen right there the year before) and halted to listen again. A tinkle came faintly from a thicket below, where maples and spruce crowded the creek. We forced our way through dense brush to find cows still browsing though the sun was low.

"I'm going to cross the creek," Laurance shouted. "You stay here. Head 'em off as they come. Try to turn 'em toward the hill." Boob plunged into the creek. Mabe and I were left alone. Shadows lay around us. I heard Boob crash through the bushes, then my brother's shout, "Here she comes. Don't let 'er get away." A big Guernsey humped across the creek and started up the hill, then stopped to placidly crop grass. Other cows splashed across and moved up the hill, grazing. Bloomy's bell sounded, deep in the swamp. Suddenly there was a jangle and she came waddling across the creek. Boob followed, big feet spattering water in sheets, Laurance triumphant on her back. "I got 'em all," he said.

Bloomy moved to the head of the line and the others followed, stirring up dust. From their tongues glistened long strings of saliva as they threw back their heads to swipe clouds of black flies clustered on their shoulders. A delicious scent of dung and milk-filled udders rose from their bodies. At the stable Cousin Percy lighted the lantern. He tossed the match into the wet gutter and lowered the globe. The flame cuddled down on the wick and purred. He started to milk while Laurance and I fed the horses and rubbed them down.

When the chores were done we all went in to supper. After supper Cousin Loraine put the kerosene lamp on the living room table and began to play the piano. Laurance and I stood on each side of her to sing while Cousin Percy lounged back in his stocking feet and joined us.

Cousin Loraine wouldn't let us stay overnight. "Aunt Emma'll worry," she said. "We don't have a phone, you know." Pockets full of cookies, we started out in the darkness. Before the first stone wall our eyes had grown used to the dark. We knew every house along the way and every herd of cows and team of horses in the pastures. The shape of every rock was familiar.

As we tiptoed upstairs Aunt Emma roused and met us in the hall. "You shouldn't have bothered Loraine," she chided.

"She wanted us to stay," I said.

"We helped Cousin Percy with the chores," said Laurance.

"Well—"

She smoothed the sheets around our faces and kissed us goodnight. From downstairs came padding footsteps and angry mutters as Uncle Fred made sure that we'd locked the door.

Laurance got a job mowing the lawn and taking care of the garden for Aunt Mary in West Bangor. I spent a week at a time at Spruce Crest Hill. Cousin Loraine furnished paper and pencil and admired my drawings. I spent hours in the stable sketching the chickens and outside watching how they lived. The red rooster had a favorite hen. While she sat on her nest under the lilacs to lay her daily egg, he stood near her, crooning. Now and then a rat came from under the barn and scuttled toward the apple tree beyond the lilacs to gather last year's seeds. His path led close to the hen's nest. Braced solidly on brass-colored feet, the rooster watched him come. I could see three dark curved feathers of his tail begin to quiver when the rat got near. With a suppliant gesture the rat paused, then scurried on past to his meal. Sometimes he sat up like a rabbit to eat a tender weed top, which he held daintily in his pink paws.

When the hen had laid an egg she stepped importantly from the nest and the rooster joined her in raucous cackles. They seemed trying to outdo each other as they shouted the news.

The calico cat Patchwork had kittens in the haymow. I lured them out and played with them while the mother cat purred in the hay beside us. I explored the pasture and clung to the tips of great boulders. I followed cowpaths through the woods. In a boggy corner, where white violets starred wet moss, I found a junco's nest with four bluish-white eggs spotted with brown. From one spruce to another the mother bird flew, uttering sharp cries of protest as I stayed for a few moments to inspect her nest.

Laurance came up to Spruce Crest Hill to help with haying. He helped load. I drove the team. In the dim, dusty mow we tramped the hay while sunbeams from knotholes crossed above us and dust particles and insects danced together.

There were pictures enough. In the barnyard I watched men drink buttermilk and horses lean eagerly to gather wisps of fallen hay; swallows wheeled overhead, to warn us with anxious twitters that their nests were in the loft.

One day I was alone with Cousin Percy when he drove Boob and Bess after the last jag of hay in a field. Dark clouds towered with a threat of rain. He spoke sharply to the horses and as they were slow to start he gathered the ends of the lines and lashed their rumps. The buckle on one end hit Boob. She gave a lunge and the team broke into a gallop. I held tight as the springless wagon jolted over the stony field.

Thunder muttered far away and a dart of light flickered among heavy blue clouds which reached steadily higher. The iron tires clanged as they bounced over ruts and boulders. "Come on!" yelled Cousin Percy as he flapped the lines. "Hee-yaw!" The horses tucked their heads and galloped faster. In the stubble field lay haycocks rounded like bee skeps.

"You drive," said Cousin Percy as we reached them. He put the lines in my hands and jumped to the ground. He stooped beside the nearest mound of hay, thrust his fork in, and swung the whole mass up on the wagon. "Tramp it," he ordered. With his fork he twirled the few wisps left, like spaghetti off a plate, and passed to the other side. His fork went in, the muscles of his arms knotted under his chambray shirt and another haycock traveled upward. It slithered into the wagon. "Next," he said as he walked on. Forkful by forkful he built the load. At each stop the horses reached to gather bunches of hay from the ground. Horseflies bit wickedly as they do before a rain. Over the far woods clouds billowed. Thunder rumbled like the moving wheels of trains.

Cousin Percy threw on the final forkful, stepped on the doubletree and put his foot on Boob's rump. He hoisted himself to the front of the load, plumped beside me and took the lines. "Hee-yaw!" Boob gave a start. Both horses lunged into their collars.

We were just ahead of the rain. Already trees had turned their leaves and bent almost double before the wind. Snatches of hay whirled from the load and went sailing off. As the horses charged across a rutted, stony field the front wheels lurched into a deep rut and stuck crosswise. The horses jolted to a stop. "Hee-yaw!" screeched Cousin Percy. He brought the ends of the lines down on Boob's rump. Bess threw herself into the collar, but with a great sigh Boob collapsed to the ground. Bess still struggled to pull, but snapped back at the dead weight.

"Get out of there!" cried Cousin Percy to Boob. He lashed down with all his strength. Boob didn't budge. She cringed as the leather stung her, but she made no move to get up. Bess lunged against the load, but she couldn't drag Boob with her. "Get up, you gol-darned bastard," Cousin Percy screamed. He lashed Boob again and again. "Here," he said and handed me feet-first down the side of the load. "Stand back." He leaped to the ground, still holding the lines, and forgetting I was there, went to work on Boob. He flailed her with the lines; kicked her flank. One tug was stretched taut across her side and the neck yoke was jammed tight against her throat while the side of her head pressed against the pole, which Bess held at an angle.

I wanted to scream, "Stop it!" but the words wouldn't come. I didn't have Mama there to speak up. She would never have stood for such a thing. I cowered and watched while Cousin Percy flung down the lines, wrenched loose a two-by-four from the wagon and held it like a club. He brought it down on Boob's rump. Whack! She cringed and groaned, but she didn't get up. Cousin Percy became a monster. He beat without mind, sometimes hitting her hip or the root of her tail with a sickening thud.

Thunder growled overhead and lightning streaked close. At last Cousin Percy threw the stake aside and unhooked Boob's traces. He undid the yoke from the pole and unsnapped the lines from Boob's bit. He rigged up Bess' harness so she could pull single and led her off at an angle. With a mighty surge she made the tires hop out of the rut. The wagon moved ahead. Cousin Percy drove from the ground. I tagged behind. Bess got the load to the barn before the first drops fell.

"What about Boob?" I asked in a small voice as rain pounded the barn roof and lightning flashed.

"She'll come in when she's good and ready. Darn stubborn fool!"

Before Bess was unhitched I heard Boob race to the barn.

Fall was potato-digging time. During the height of harvest, school was dismissed so children could help. Cousin Percy grew acres of potatoes for market, and he offered to pay us for picking up. He rigged Boob, Bess and Mabe into a three-horse team to pull a mechanical digger. The three horses struggled with all their strength to pull it, while Cousin Percy wielded a whip. The machine clattered crazily as it gouged potatoes out of the ground, threshed the dried tops and let the freed potatoes shiver back and forth on a slatted belt that tumbled them to the ground. There Laurance and I picked them up into bags.

At evening Cousin Percy hitched the team to the wagon and let Laurance drive down the rows. Cousin Percy stooped his squat figure, heaved a bag onto his shoulder and, bent over, plodded to the wagon. There he turned and flipped the bag into the wagon bed. The high-piled bags were so heavy that the horses could barely move the load across the soft field. On the hard road we climbed on, but got off at the foot of the steep hill. Cousin Percy urged the horses upward, thrashing his whip. Frantic feet scrabbled, striking sparks. Sometimes Mabe fell to her knees. I pushed with all my weight and Laurance grasped the spokes of the hind wheel and turned. The load seemed ready to tip backward onto us all.

When we reached a level place Cousin Percy cramped the front wheels, told Laurance to block the rear ones, and he let the horses breathe. Mabe's bay coat was black with sweat, and her ribs jerked in and out as she gasped for breath. Water ran down her legs and dripped off her belly, rolling away in pellets of dust. Boob and Bess breathed in short, hard gulps, ribs working like bellows, and from their bodies sweat trickled down their legs. Soon Boob and Bess breathed normally again and we started on, though Mabe wheezed and her legs trembled.

"Why does Cousin Percy make the load so heavy?" I asked Laurance.

"Well, *he* carries all he can lift. So can they."

Wintertime

THAT WINTER Laurance attended junior high school in North Bangor, six miles away. I went to West Bangor, a half mile from Aunt Emma's. In moderate weather Laurance walked to school, hitching a ride with any rig that came along. When the temperature was 10° to 20° below zero he rode the mail sleigh, getting to school any time the mailman arrived in North Bangor. By afternoon more sleighs were on the road and he could find a ride home.

The roads were kept open by snowplows drawn by teams. One morning Aunt Clara called up the stairs, "Laurance, Hope, come quick. Something's coming down the road." We raced downstairs in our nightgowns. A strange outfit approached. George Bartram's heavy team of bays came struggling through snowdrifts that reached their bellies. Behind them a huge black cast-iron syrup kettle jerked along, swaying and bobbing. In the kettle stood Mr. Bartram. His feet were braced wide and he held tight to the lines to keep from falling. He was bundled to the ears in mackinaw and scarf. In the cold air he and his horses shot breath like steam from their nostrils.

The peculiar rig went floundering by the house while Aunt Clara, Uncle Fred, Aunt Emma and we children gawked. "Beats all I ever saw," cried Aunt Clara, her hooked nose flat against the pane.

"The man's crazy," sputtered Uncle Fred. "That kettle's not going to open the road."

"George Bartram always was a bright child," said Aunt Emma. "When I had him in school he was full of clever ideas. Who else would've though to break road with a syrup kettle!"

"Boy, I'd like to take a ride in that," said Laurance. "Look how it jogs around without turning over. I'm going out and see what kind of track it makes."

We got on our clothes and waded through deep snow out to the roadside. Leading toward South Bangor lay a broad, wobbly trough with rounded bottom, smooth and white in the three-foot-deep snow. Far up the track wavered George Bartram's outlandish contraption, crawling like a black bug through the snow.

Two hours later the kettle plowed past in the opposite direction to make another groove. When Mr. Striker came through with the mail his horse trotted and his sleigh runners slid lightly in the kettle tracks. Laurance hopped aboard and rode to school. I walked down the smooth path to West Bangor without getting snow in my overshoes.

Lawrence folks lived everywhere in that north country. My favorite Lawrence on the way to Cousin Percy's was Cousin Hazel, who had married my Cousin Jess. One winter day I planned to help her shell beans while Laurance was going to work with Cousin Jess in the woods. They sky was gray with a milky sun just risen as we knocked on the door. Cousin Jess was sprawled at the head of the big oil-cloth–covered table, looking across the road to his barn. Their three young sons dressed by the fire. "Light and set," said Cousin Jess.

Cousin Hazel turned another batch of pancakes and poured her husband a second cup of Postum. "You hain't et yet, have you?" She whisked plates onto the table and stacked them high with cakes. Cousin Jess handed the butter and shoved a tin pail of maple syrup down the table. "Help yourselves," he said.

We lathered the cakes with butter and swamped them with syrup. Cousin Hazel's slippered feet sluffed from table to stove and back as she fried more eggs and poured hot water into our cups. She disappeared down cellar to come up with a jar of raspberry preserves wrapped in her apron. "Here's something special," she said, as she wiped off dust. "I saved this for you kids. See if it tastes good." We piled it on top of the syrup. Harvey, Donald and Wayne finished dressing and came to the table to wolf their food. At last Cousin Hazel had a chance to sit down. "My, it was a dinger last night," she remarked. "Weren't you fellows cold coming up?"

"We kept moving," said Laurance.

"Eat all you want," urged Cousin Jess. He gazed out the window. "It's going to snow," he said. "If we hurry maybe we can get a good bit of wood before she comes."

Laurance gobbled his last bite and got into his things. Cousin Jess, bundled in mackinaw and wool cap, said to

Cousin Hazel, "We'll work till noon if it doesn't snow. Water the cows before you get into anything else."

When she and I were through eating we put on our clothes to go water the cows, and get the beans. "You young'uns behave," she warned the boys, who dawdled at the table. "Harvey, clear the table and keep the fire going, and see the others don't get into mischief." We went out. The sun peered from a veil of snow-mist. A gust of wind whipped the barn door from Cousin Hazel's hands as she tried to open it. "Whew, we're in for another blizzard," she said as she wrenched it open with both hands. "Seems like we'd had enough." Snow lay over the fields almost to the fence tops, and was banked high against the sides of the barn. Inside the stable we released the cows, then followed them out through the barnlot to the wooded stream a quarter mile away.

The watering hole, cut through thick ice the day before, was frozen over. She chopped it open with an ax. At each stroke the ax hit water and came up sheathed with a fresh layer of ice until it had grown almost too heavy to lift. The cows crowded near. "That ought to do 'em," said Cousin Hazel as she dragged away the unwieldy ax. The first cow plunged her nose among floating ice cakes and began to drink. The others jostled each other to take turns. We went back to get the beans.

In fall the beans had been picked when dry and brought into the hay barn. They lay in mounds on the floor between the mows. Cousin Hazel and I each filled a bushel basket with the stiff crackly pods and carried them in to the kitchen. We set them down beside the cookstove, where the teakettle purred. In the other room by the heater the boys were playing.

"Just let me stir up some cookies," said Cousin Hazel. She hustled her things off and slipped into an apron, opened the stove lid and pushed in wood. I sat down to the beans. I ran my thumb slowly down the edge of a pod, pressed hard, and made two halves part like an opening zipper to spill out six white beans. They were marrows, emerging fat and clean from the dirty gray pod. My task became a rhythm as I took a pod, pressed it open, and let beans patter into the pan on my lap.

The teakettle sang; Cousin Hazel's wooden spoon went swish, swish around the bowl; from outdoors came the sound of the wind, which now whirled bunches of snow against the window.

The first pan of cookies went in and Cousin Hazel took a seat and began to shell. "Listen to that wind, huh? Hope the boys don't get stuck." Her nimble hands sent a cascade of beans into her pan. "For dinner we'll have peas and mashed potatoes. I'll open a can of those sweet pickles you and Laurance like." Every few minutes she jumped up to tend her cookies, keeping the stove stuffed with wood. After a while one end of the table was heaped with fragrant spice cookies cooling on a white cloth.

Wind shook the panes and cold air forced its way in around the frames. Snow fell so thick that I couldn't see across the road. Dinner time came. Still Laurance and Cousin Jess hadn't come.

While I cut bread there came a stamp of heavy feet on the porch. The door burst inward and with it Cousin Jess on a blast of frigid air. He slammed the door against the wind. "No more work today," he said, as he shook snow from his cap onto the mat.

"Ain't Laurance with you?" asked Cousin Hazel. She

ladled butter over the peas.

"He'll be here. Took the team over to water 'em at Spauldings."

"Oh, Jess! You shouldn't have let him. He'll get lost in this blizzard."

"Shucks. The horses know the way home if he don't." He moved to the washbasin and splashed water over his face. He sat down to the table, his eyes on the howling snow outside.

We started to eat. Cousin Hazel fidgeted and looked out the window with every bite she took. Ten minutes later I heard a commotion from the wagonshed off the side porch.

"What on earth—" Cousin Jess jumped up. He strode to the door and flung it wide. Laurance stumbled past him, eyebrows frosty, clothes grizzled. "Made it!" he announced, and peered around the kitchen as though it were a foreign country. His eyebrows were white as an old man's.

Cousin Jess went out the door. Laurance removed his things and Cousin Hazel shook off the snow and hung them on chairs beside the stove.

"Boy, I thought my hands would freeze," he said as he sat down.

"This food'll warm you up," said Cousin Hazel, as she filled his plate. "Here, drink some hot Postum."

Cousin Jess came back. "It's wicked out there," he said. "Glad we got that wood out this morning."

Laurance began his story. "Well, headed for Spauldings and the wind at our backs sort of blew us along. But the minute we veered west the wind hit the horses right in the face. They turned tail and plunged off the road into a drift." He chewed a while. "I couldn't tell where they were headed, so I grabbed Maude's tail and hung on. We wallowed through that drift, hit a fence and went along it for a while, then got back on the road. We finally made the watering trough. I broke the ice so's they could drink and we headed home. Couldn't see a thing. Just hung onto Maude's tail with my scarf clear over my eyes. I kept hanging on, figuring the horses would lead me to the barn.

"All at once they swerved into some kind of building. I didn't know it was the wagonshed till I pulled down my scarf and cast my eyes around. The horses acted crazy. They bumped into a wagon, then into that old mower. It puzzled me why they were acting that way. I went to their heads and found the reason. Their eyes were sealed shut! I took off my mittens and started melting snow with my hands. Had to scratch ice away with my fingernails."

He chuckled. "That's the first time I ever healed the blind by laying on of hands."

One February morning Cousin Percy said. "Want to come with me to the woods? I've got to find a new runner for my sugar sled."

The sled with which he gathered maple sap was like a stoneboat, with runners made of ironwood, hickory or beech. "Got to find a sapling curved just right," he said as we trod the snow. He had an ax over his shoulder. It was a bright cold morning. I stepped in Cousin Percy's deep, wide-spaced tracks, as his short powerful legs worked steadily up the slope toward the sugarbush.

This side of the stand of ancient sugar maples stretched

a growth of younger trees—birch, cherry and soft maple, sprinkled through with hardwood saplings. Here the snow lay less deep, exposing tree boles almost to the ground. A few chickadees had joined us the moment we stepped into the woods. They flew ahead with their "dee-dee-dees" as if showing us the way.

Cousin Percy stopped beside the twisty gray trunk of an eight-inch ironwood. "This here's a likely one," he said. "Look at that crook at the base." He trained his eyes on the smooth-barked trunk, which spiraled upward through competing maple and birch. "Stem's crooked as a ram's horn. It's a mite too small, too. I think we can do better."

We tramped from tree to tree. The hickories all grew straight as lodgepoles. "If I aimed to find a straight one they'd all be crooknecks," said Cousin Percy. Only the hard gray ironwoods had bent knees, and their trunks wound up like corkscrews. We marched down the aisles of straight young trees and came to the spruce forest along the creek. White birches rose like slender threads against the dark tapestry of spruce.

Close beside the path Cousin Percy found what he was looking for. "This is the one," he said. "See that crook at the bottom?" A hickory about ten inches through made a sharp bend after leaving the ground, then grew straight, as though pulled from above. "Cows made this one for us." Cousin Percy grinned. "Must've stepped on this when it was little, but it wouldn't stay down." He cut some brush around the tree and swept snow from the base. "Stand back," he said. With a few swift ax strokes he cut the tree at ground level. Soon the branches were lopped off a fifteen-foot length and the tree chopped in two.

"Isn't that too long?" I asked.

"What's over I'll season for ax handles. Say, suppose you can carry my ax?" He handed me the big double-bitted ax and shouldered the heavy timber, steadying it with both hands. "I should cure this but I need that runner right now."

At the barn Cousin Percy laid the section of hickory beside the sugar sled with its one sound runner. "A good match," he said. He used the old runner as a model and hewed the timber roughly into shape with the ax. After a break for dinner he worked with a drawshave to get it smooth and flat. The natural curve made a turned-up front end. With heavy-duty bolts he fastened it in place. "A good day's work," he said. "It's time for milking."

Early on a Sunday in March we started to tap. Banks of snow were still heaped high in the woods. "Tree roots know it's spring," said Cousin Percy. "Sap's started to rise."

We rode to the sugarhouse on the bobsled behind Boob and Bess. Cousin Percy stood in front. Laurance and I sat on the back, so our legs could swing, our feet scuff snow. The bobsled runners left gleaming marks like snail tracks in the sun.

At the sugarhouse Cousin Percy creaked the door open. We entered the dim room where light fell from the cupola and sifted through knotholes. The big vat sat on its brick foundation and stacks of tin pails lined the walls. Cousin Percy lifted the cover of a wooden box and took out a curved metal spout. "Guess we have plenty of spiles," he said. He had a brace and bit in his hand. "I'll start tapping. Laurance, you bring a bunch of pails. Here, Hope, carry this box of spiles."

We went on foot, leaving the team tied near the shanty. At the first big maple Cousin Percy set the point of the drill to the rough trunk and bored in; flakes of bark scattered like sawdust. When the bit reached live wood a curl of white corkscrewed out. With it came a trickle of sap which ran down to soak the bark. I had a spile ready. He took a hammer from his belt and tapped the spile in firmly. Now sap bubbled out through the spout in a tiny stream mixed with bits of wood. Laurance hung a pail on the spout and the first drops tinked onto the bottom.

Meanwhile Cousin Percy had gone around the other side of the tree and bored another hole. Big trees with big crowns could handle two, he said. We moved over mounds and ridges among the leafless trees. Pretty soon Laurance said to me, "Let's go back to that first one." We dropped pails and spouts and ran. Laurance got there first and unhooked the pail. He tipped it, threw back his head, and poured the sap down his gullet.

"Leave me some," I said. "You're going to finish it."

"Here—baby. Plenty left." He handed me the pail as he wiped his mouth on his mitten. A film of sap lay over the bottom. I raised the cold sticky edge to my mouth and up-ended the pail. Pale as water, but tinged with sweetness, the maple sap caressed my throat. I spit out bits of wood and bark that stuck to my tongue.

We children took off school for sugaring. Aunt Emma let us stay up at Cousin Percy's for two whole weeks. All through the woods seeped the tang of dry wood burning and the fragrant steam of boiling sap. While Cousin Percy drove the sled with its great tank, we scurried from one tapped tree to another and trudged through drifts with brimming pails, to dump into the tank.

On crackling cold mornings the sled stuck fast whenever it stopped. Boob and Bess had to make more than one start, and when the runner jarred loose the sap slopped over the top of the tank.

"Boy, all that sap wasted," mourned Laurance. "After it came drop by drop and we carried it in buckets, it pours out by the gallon!"

The second week brought mild weather. Crows called as they flew over. One night we had a "sugar snow," big lazy flakes that floated down. "That brings the sap up," said Cousin Percy. The snow soon melted off in bright gurgling rills. Old drifts thawed. Woods and fields were full of melted water lying in pools. In many places the sled slithered over leaves and dead twigs instead of snow.

When Laurance and I were back in school we still walked up Sundays to help gather. April was almost over when Cousin Percy said, "This'll be the last run. Sap's getting buddy." It did have a bitter taste. The day was so warm that a lot of flies and moths lay drowned in the sap buckets. While the last batch evaporated Laurance and I went the rounds to pull out spiles and plug each hole with a dowel so the tree could heal.

Now that sugaring was over, folks had time for more sugar parties. We children ate wax-on-snow until our stomachs ached, then downed pickles so we could eat more.

A week after sugaring Laurance and I went to Spruce Crest Hill to explore. We found two dogs tied to an old wagon beside the barn. Before we entered the yard they heard us and tossed at the ends of their chains, barking. They were giants. "Belgian police dogs," said Cousin Percy. "Guy in the city brought 'em here. Just pups.

Gentle as kittens. Go over and pat 'em."

They barked ferociously, but when we went near they licked our hands and whined, wagging their tails."

"You going to keep 'em?" asked Laurance.

"Don't aim to. Your Cousin Bennett wants that dark one; I'll give the other away." I was petting the creamy white one whose name was Buff.

"Maybe we can have him!" I said.

"Let's write and ask Mama," said Laurance. "She'll be up soon and we can take him back with us."

"I have to keep 'em chained or they devil the cows," said Cousin Percy. "You kids can take 'em for a walk if you want."

Buff was so strong I could hardly hold him. He leaped wildly, almost knocking me down, but he didn't snap or snarl. The two dogs led us at break-neck speed down the pasture trails, where blackberry thorns tore my legs and stones bruised my feet.

We wrote to Mama. She wrote back, "I'll be up next week to get you. See the good news in my letter to Aunt Emma. About the dog—we'll see when I get there."

Tamarack Farm

The news in Mama's letter was that she'd bought another farm. It was bigger than Apple Tree Lane Farm. It had a stream right back of the house. There was a stand of old timber and lots of open space. "Wait till you see the sun setting over the trees!" she wrote.

Vivid pictures came to my mind. Maybe we could have a horse again, since Tom was now at Aunt Emma's. I'd farm the place myself, while Mama and Laurance worked out. Joe was no longer living with us. He had gone out west with Papa and didn't come back for five years, and then only to visit. At sixteen Laurance was trying to save up money to attend the parochial academy Mama insisted on. She didn't want either of us to attend public school.

She had bought an automobile too—an old Willys-Knight touring car. In May she drove up to get us.

In the kitchen that evening she told her plans, while Uncle Fred sat morosely in the living room and Aunt

Clara and Aunt Emma leaned their arms on the kitchen table and took in every word. "It's seventy acres," Mama exclaimed, her eyes shining. "The fields are run down, but with proper care they can be brought back. There's a big stand of pine and hemlock I can sell if worse comes to worst. With the Willys I can drive to Cleveland, only two miles away, to give lessons or hang paper—maybe even sell baked goods again."

"I'll run the farm," I said.

"I'm afraid it'll be a long time before we can afford a horse, or tools," she said. "But you'll be in the country, like you want. And you can earn money picking berries. There's lots of huckleberries around there. Some farmers raise strawberries. Laurance can work on the road and save money for school. Maybe this fall."

"Oh boy!" said Laurance. "I'll save all I can, and at school I'll work most of my way." He juggled three spoons in the air.

"We'll see," said Mama. "The owner gave a long-term mortgage so the payments aren't too high. I hope we can manage so's you can go at last."

"If I save enough money I'll go to school too," I said. "I want to study writing and drawing."

"Bide your time," said Mama. "It's Laurance's turn first."

"I'll get a horse," I said. "Then I can raise crops to sell."

A secret plan was in my mind. I knew one horse we might be able to afford. I had ridden and driven Mabe so much that she already seemed like mine. Maybe Cousin Percy would sell her. He'd said she wasn't much use to him anymore, with her heaves getting worse. He had a car now and didn't need a buggy horse. She just roamed the pasture all summer and stood in her stall all winter. He'd never sell her to a stranger.

Mama slept with me, and before we went to sleep I asked her about Mabe, and reminded her she'd almost promised us Buff.

"We'll see. Now let me sleep."

For three days Mama visited with Aunt Emma and all our other kin. On the last day she drove up to see Cousin Percy and Cousin Loraine. She said nothing about the horse and I didn't dare keep at her. She fell in love with Buff, though, and said we could have him. "I'll feel safer if you children have a dog," she said.

Before we left I said goodbye to Cousin Loraine's cats and I hugged Mabe's patient face and kissed her black velvet nose. "I hope you'll be mine," I whispered. I didn't have much hope, Mama'd just bought the car; there was the mortgage; and now Laurance would be going to school.

Could I ever earn enough to buy a horse? I thought of my drawing. I'd been painting with water-colors at Aunt Emma's and she had praised my pictures. I'd made Christmas cards for relatives. Maybe I could make some and sell them. But I hated to sell. I'd better stick to berries at so much a quart. If only Mama would buy Mabe my money could go to help feed her and buy tools for the farm.

After we got in the car and were almost to Norwood, Mama cleared her throat and began, "Hope, I've got some news for you." She drove for a ways while my eyes focused on the back of her neck. "While I was at Percy's I talked about buying Mabe. We dickered and he agreed to let me have her for $25 if I'd promise to keep her till she dies. He threw in a driving harness, a work harness and the buggy. You're going to have your horse."

The passing scenery blurred before my eyes.

"How'll we get her?" asked Laurance from the front seat.

"Oh, Percy knows a trucker who'll be driving our way empty and he'll bring Mabe and the buggy and all. It won't cost much, as he's got a return load."

We questioned Mama about the farm. She said, "Wait and see." In the car we traversed in less than a day the miles Mama and I had traveled during a whole week with Tom. There were no stops along the way. In mid-afternoon we drove along a dirt road with a few tumble-down deserted houses, miles and miles of worked-out fields grown up to saplings and brush. On either side old snow lay in the ditches. "We're almost there," said Mama. She hitched forward in her seat and gripped the wheel tighter. "You'll soon see Tamarack Farm." Her voice sounded the same as it had when she'd told us of Apple Tree Lane Farm years before.

On a wooden bridge we crossed a stream that flowed dark and still among bare alders. A forest of pines towered beyond. On the left appeared more brushland with a few scraggling apple trees, then a huge ghost of a barn, half the roof fallen in. A big unpainted house sprawled behind a wide lawn covered with brown grass in bunches. In the center of the barren lawn stood two leafless trees.

The Willys slowed down. Mama turned into the horseshoe drive. "Welcome to Tamarack Farm," she said and shut off the motor.

Laurance bounded out, Buff with him, and I followed. "Where are the tamaracks?" I asked.

"There, stupid," he said, and pointed to the two lifeless-looking trees in the yard.

"They don't have needles."

"Silly, don't you know they drop their needles in fall? They look like evergreens, but they're deciduous. They've got cones, though, like pines. Hey, let's go to the creek," he said, and started to run down the hill past the barn.

"Laurance," called Mama. "Come help unload the car. You can go to the creek later." She glanced around. "Look at the apple trees, children. They're already budded. And the lilacs here by the well. I hope there's a white one, but it's too early to tell."

We stepped over broken boards of a porch with leaning pillars. Mama opened the door into a great old-fashioned farm kitchen. The floor boards too were broken in places. "I'm going to get Uncle Lewis to help fix up the place," said Mama briskly. "See, I've already moved our furniture in." It was our old kitchen table which stood there, with chairs worn by our use. In the living room the library table stood between two windows and the sofa and chairs were ours.

"It's a nice big kitchen," said Mama. "I can do lots of baking here. And you children can work on your hobbies right here by the kitchen stove. Come on back, now, and get the rest of the things. I've got bedding and we can sleep in our own beds tonight."

Mama showed us our upstairs rooms with their rough splintery floors and big windows with tiny panes. Mine looked out on the road toward town. From Laurance's, you could see the creek, and beyond to the pasture with patches of trees and brush and a corner of the pine-woods. Down the hall was a low-ceilinged unfinished bedroom where a dormer window had been cut and never completed. Mama had set up her bedstead there. "Pshaw, I'm never in my room except to sleep," she said. "I want you each to have a room where you can keep your things. I'll have Uncle Lewis make closets and Laurance can put up shelves. The small bedroom downstairs will be for guests, or a boarder if I get one." After Mama'd showed us the pantry and the cellar she let us go.

We looked into the barn with its great empty bays. Below, a rickety door opened on a musty stable with a dirt floor. "I'll put Mabe in here," I said. "But dirt won't be good, will it?"

"Some people use it," said Laurance. He poked about the dark interior where mangers and partitions had been wrenched out and not even a scrap of harness hung on the rusty nails. "If I get money, I'll pour concrete," he offered. "I can make forms and have gutters and everything, if you want to keep a cow. I'd put four-inch planks over the concrete for the animals to stand on."

"Could you make a stanchion for the cow?"

"I could make the frame. You can buy the stanchion second-hand. If we get boards and two-by-fours I can make dandy mangers. You'd better ask Mama to get the planks right away. I'll put 'em over the dirt, slanted front to back for drainage. You don't want Mabe standing in mud. When we put in concrete I'll just switch the boards to the top."

"How'll I tie her?"

"I'll get a ring somewhere and nail it into that beam. Maybe Uncle Lewis has an old ring. You can put hay on the floor till we get a manger. Boy, are you lucky! You've got a horse, and a harness and buggy. That's more'n I ever had. But I don't really care. I'll be driving the car pretty soon. And I'm going to spend my spare time on my invention. It'll be the first three-wheeled auto ever made."

"You'll be going to school," I said. "I wish I could go."

"Keep your shirt on," he said. "Your turn'll come. Hey, let's go down to the creek!"

A wagon path led to the water, which flowed swiftly from a smother of alders to run past remnants of a broken-down bridge. Rotted timbers lay half buried in weed stalks and blackberry canes. Around two weathered posts swirled the current. Faint wagon tracks led into the water and out the other side, up a slope to the pasture. Laurance and I took off sneakers and socks and waded in. A school of minnows darted to the shelter of the alders. Over our white feet shadows moved as water striders skipped along the surface. Tree swallows wheeled over our heads and swept low over the alders.

"We can swim here," Laurance said as we splashed across. "I'll build a dam down below."

"If we have a pond, we can have waterlilies," I said. "I've seen where you can send away and get roots. I want pink and white and yellow."

Laurance scrabbled up the far bank, me after him, and then Buff. Laurance had his knife and was on the lookout for a slingshot crotch. My mind appraised the farm. The ground was sand and gravel, with patches of stones. Mats of dry moss were everywhere, interspersed with clumps of tough poverty grass. It wasn't like Grandpa's farm. It wasn't even like Apple Tree Lane Farm. With all these acres, though, a horse and a cow might find enough to eat. I would build a fence.

We raced through the pasture to a grove of giant beeches among which grew hemlock and soft maple. Against the dark hemlock boughs the smooth gray beech and maple stood in relief. Last year's tawny leaves dangled from slender twigs, to make a design on the dark background. I peered through a lattice of branches to the shady depths of the grove.

"Come on," called Laurance. He pranced ahead until he found the slingshot crotch he wanted. He notched the sapling and removed the center crotch. "This would have made a perfect goldfinch nest site," he said. "But there's plenty more. I'll bet there'll be goldfinches all over here, and redstarts in the grove and catbirds and thrushes down by the creek."

"Will you put up birdhouses?"

"Sure. Soon as we find lumber. Look at those tree swallows." We lifted our faces to the sky where swallows soared. "All they need is holes to nest in."

"How about bluebirds?"

"There must be hollows in those old apple trees. But they can use some of the boxes too."

We had reached a ridge at the top of the long pasture slope. On a mat of dry moss we flopped to look back on the way we'd come. Through scattered saplings we could see over the tips of the alders a portion of the house, in which Mama was arranging our belongings. To one side the upper part of the barn looked like a gray fortress long deserted.

"With Mabe I'm going to work the farm," I said.

"Do what you want," said Laurance as he whittled his slingshot into shape. "I can't help you. I'm going to work out for money, not farm."

"But you promised to make the stable floor."

"Well, sure. But Mama'll have to get the stuff to do it with."

"I know. And I can make a fence myself, if she'll get the wire. I'll begin to cut posts tomorrow."

"I'm going to start on my three-wheeler." He jumped up. "I'll race you back to the barn."

The next day I hurried with the ax to the woods, where at the edge I cut slender stuff which would make two or three posts to a tree. I dragged the poles together in bunches, to stockpile them ready for Mabe to skid out. In the barn I sketched an elaborate picture of the stable. Purposely I made the picture gloomy and I called it "The Empty Stall." I planned a sequel which would show Mabe standing there, bedding under her and hay in a manger. I would call it "The New Tenant."

Mabe arrived. She walked down the shaky gangplank and without hesitation put her muzzle to the grass and started to graze. The driver slid the gangplank back into his truck, slammed the tailgate shut. Mama paid him and he drove off. "Well, you've got your horse now," she said. "I hope you're satisfied."

"I am." Suddenly a kaleidoscope of all I wanted flashed before me. Its immensity overwhelmed me. "Mama, we need hay and oats," I said. "And I'll have to have wire and staples for the fence."

"I've only got so much money," she said with a sigh. "The house has to be fixed livable." She watched Mabe biting the short grass. "Of course she's got to eat. I'll go down in the Willys today and get a bale of hay and a bag of oats to tide her over till the grass grows. I can't get the wire yet. Not till I find some jobs. But you can tie her around the yard. We've got a rope."

I got the long rope and tied it to Mabe's halter and

tethered her to a maple near the barn. In her stable I put dry grass and dead leaves for bedding. When Mama unloaded a bale of hay and a bag of oats I asked, "How about the boards for the floor? And I need a manger for the hay. Laurance said he'd make it if you got lumber."

Her face clouded. "That's all I can do right now!" she said. "You'll just have to wait."

Later I put Mabe in the stable and groomed her while she ate. "You're mine," I crooned. She bent an ear back to listen. "You're mine and you always will be. I'll love you forever." After I'd combed and brushed her to a good shine I led her to the creek. Her black muzzle sent water in waves that disturbed the water striders and frightened the minnows. I knelt beside her and while waves slapped the shore I thanked God for giving me Mabe.

The summer's road work had already begun and Laurance got a job on the crew. He would make three dollars a day. Before daylight he walked out to where he could get a ride on one of the trucks. After dark he walked home.

I worked alone. I cut the trimmed poles into post-lengths and sharpened the smaller ends. I stood on a chair to pound the posts in, and there was Mabe's fence. It began at the creek, ran uphill to enclose the barn, and thence over near the house, to jog behind and go back down to the creek. On the far side of the ford I piled timbers to make a barrier Mabe wouldn't cross.

Now for the wire. Mama had established a bakery route and the kitchen was full of pans of bread rising, cookie dough in bowls and pies cooling on shelves. I wanted to help her earn money, but she didn't need me.

I tried washing dishes but my eyes were out the window, my mind on the farm.

"Oh, leave the dishes," she said sharply. "I'd rather do them myself than watch you do it. Go out and do whatever you want." With relief I lifted my hands from the soapy water, leaped upstairs to get pad and pencil and went out. I used colored pencils to put in brown earth, green poplars and flaming red of a maple whose seeds were bright as flowers.

When Mama got back from her baked-goods route I asked again for wire.

Mama wrestled a huge bowl down from the shelf. Her face had the closed look I dreaded. As she placed the bowl on the table her expression changed to one of resignation. "How much wire will you need?"

"About 1500 feet."

"That's a lot of fence," Mama said as she measured warm water into the bowl and added yeast. With both hands she scooped flour from a fifty-pound bag and dumped it in. She took a big steel spoon and started to mix.

"Well, I was going to get linoleum for your room," she said. "Would you rather have the fence?"

"Yes. I don't need linoleum."

Mama bought the wire and staples. As I unrolled the wire along the line of posts it sprang into spirals. When I tried to pull it tight it snapped my fingers and gouged a hole in my leg. That night at supper I asked Laurance if he'd help me.

"Can't do it now," he said. "Maybe on Sunday. But I'd hoped to work all day on my three-wheeler."

That Sunday the fence was finished by noon. The

posts were small but the wire was tight. I put Mabe in her new pasture and watched her put her nose to the grass.

"You're free." I said.

Mama got an old set of one-horse tools and I hitched Mabe to the plow. She struggled to pull the plow through interlaced roots of quack grass and perennial weeds. Finally the garden was harrowed and ready to plant. In the roughest spots I put in potatoes, corn and beans. Near the house I raked a plot for radishes, lettuce, beets, carrots and onions.

"I won't neglect the garden," I told Mama. "I love to work in the dirt."

"Not me," said Laurance. "I love to eat vegetables, not grow 'em. I'd rather shovel hot tar all day." He was proud of his muscles. At thirteen I still loved horses above everything else.

Laurance helped me make birdhouses. We put some on the fence posts and nailed others to old apple trees. Tree swallows took some of the houses, bluebirds the others. As I walked the pasture I saw either a tree swallow or a bluebird peek from each house. Laurance had put one house high on the clothespole beside the house, next to the garden. A pair of bluebirds moved in. As I hoed and weeded they warbled, and they sat on stakes that marked the rows and dropped into fresh-stirred earth for insects. About the size of a sparrow, the male moved in a blaze of blue, and when he perched, his brick-red breast and white underparts made a colorful picture. One day as I leaned on my hoe I heard a whir of wings and something landed on my head. I moved, and with a cry the male bluebird flew away while my scalp felt the dig of his take-off. When I told Laurance he laughed. "He thought you were a post. A natural mistake."

On Sabbath, when we didn't have to work, Laurance and I took long rambles, as we used to do when we lived at Apple Tree Lane Farm. We explored swamps and woodlands, found birds' nests and waded streams. Laurance took careful notes and I made sketches.

Mama was of two minds about my love for nature, and the way I kept drawing more instead of less. "You're going to be like your father," she warned. "It was his love for nature that drew me to him, but nature is only the reflection of God. We must look above, and get ready for the next world."

"But Mama, if God made birds and flowers, if we love them don't we worship Him?" For me, the New Jerusalem with streets of gold did not attract like a green lawn ablaze with dandelions. And how could angels' music outdo the robin's song?

"Love not the world, nor the things that are in the world," she quoted. Mama believed what she said, but the sight of earthly beauty was everything to me.

"Your father turned away from God," she said. "Now he's wandering and lost. And he's taken Joe with him." Her face was sad. "I won't have that happen to you and Laurance. I'm going to send you to a Christian school."

Laurance and I had been puzzled about something for a long time, and now Laurance brought it up. "Mama, how about the time Joe and I climbed on the barn roof and you told us God showed us to you. Was that really true?"

"I guess you're old enough to tell now," she said with a sheepish grin. "A neighbor drove by when you were up on the ridgepole and when he saw me in McConnellsville he told me."

Laurance gasped. "Then you told a—"

"No, it wasn't a lie," Mama said emphatically. "God has His ways of working with men. I felt that neighbor was God's messenger, sent to warn me my boys were in danger. And for years your fear of God kept you safe when I had to be away."

The Letter

It was Mama's commitment to give us a Christian education that was keeping Laurance and me from school. Laurance was seventeen and should have been almost through high school. At fourteen I should have started. But we couldn't go until we had board and room and tuition, or at least enough so we could work out the rest.

On rainy days I read and reread the books we had: Louisa May Alcott's *Little Women* from mama's childhood; Fox's *Book of Martyrs*; *Pilgrim's Progress* by John Bunyan; and a few others. Above all I cherished the books Papa had sent: Ernest Thompson Seton's *Wild Animals I Have Known*, *Wild Animals at Home*, and *Two Little Savages*. Every story of Seton's brought tears to my eyes. My favorite was "The Pacing Mustang." I decided that when winter came I would copy every sketch and full-page plate in *Wild Animals at Home*.

Inspite of Mama's fears, I took care of the garden.

Cultivating was not so hard on Mabe as plowing. Up and down the rows with a skillful turn at the end, we established a camaraderie that Laurance couldn't understand.

"What do you see in that old nag?"

"I love her. What do you see in those bolts and junk you call an auto?"

"I'm inventing something. Something great you couldn't even dream of."

"Mabe's a living creature invented by God," I said.

"Well, God invented me and gave me a brain. So what I invent with it is His work, isn't it?"

Once the days grew frosty, Laurance's road job was done. I listened as he and Mama discussed the family finances. "I'm sorry," said Mama. "I couldn't save enough money to start you in school. I can hardly keep up with the payments on the place. I guess you'll have to wait another year."

"That's all right, Mama," said Laurance. He sprawled on the couch, his hands clenched between his knees. "I'll work this winter. Can I cut firewood in our woods?"

"Yes, I don't see what else you can do. I'll try to find customers on my route."

"We can maybe borrow a wagon," Laurance said. He sat up. "I can deliver it with Mabe. Green wood's three dollars a cord, delivered. I bet I can cut and split a cord a day. We won't burn near that much, so I can sell some."

"Well, do what you can."

I had been left out of the discussion. What I'd earned picking berries went for Mabe's feed, and my vegetables were only a patch on what we needed for our own use. Winter was upon us and there was no hay in the barn. "What about Mabe?" I asked.

"That's right," said Mama. "Somehow we've got to feed her. You work with Laurance in the woods. You can cut together, and share. Now that summer's over I'll be getting more piano lessons. That'll help out." She was deep in thought. "How about your father?" she said to me. "Why don't you ask him to help with Mabe's keep? She's your horse."

Papa and I had been writing regularly. I sent him my best sketches and he criticized them. His letters were short in answer to my outpourings. Each ended, "Hastily, with love—" so that I expected next time he'd write more. I said little about farm work or family happenings, but gave detailed reports on birds and my drawings.

I remembered the time he'd said he'd buy me the most beautiful horse in the world if I would come to live with him. Now I told him about Mabe and how much I loved her. I explained that she needed food. At the end of my letter I put the usual message of love, with hugs and kisses.

Two weeks later the answer came. I sat at the table in my room to open it, afraid of what he would say. On the single sheet was a brief note: "—and so, I can't send money for your horse. She's not for your own pleasure, but a slavey to do the work. I told you once that if you were with me you'd have the best horse available, just for you to ride. But not while you're with your mother.

"Another thing, I hope you'll understand when I say you're too old now for the 'Gimmes.' Until you can write me, well, just because a father's a father and a daughter's a daughter, then you needn't write at all. Hastily, with love—"

My cheeks burned. Through a mist I gazed out the

window onto the bare fall fields where Mabe and I had worked so hard. Thoughts scraped inside my head like a spoon stirring dough. My eyes fell on the creased letter and torn envelope.

With fury I kicked the table leg, grabbed the papers and smashed them into a ball. I ran downstairs to put them in the kitchen stove so I'd never see them again. Mama was in the kitchen. She'd seen me go upstairs with the letter. "Did you hear from your father, dear?" she asked as she folded a circle of raw crust and placed it on top of a pie. She began to pinch the edge.

"Yes, I got a letter." I held the lid off for a moment while the edges curled crisply, gray under a bright flame, and the letter fell to ashes. I slammed the lid back on.

"What did he say about feed?" she asked as she put the finished pie aside and began another crust.

"He can't send anything," I said.

"Well, I didn't think so. At least you asked."

"I'm going outdoors," I said and rushed outside. Mabe was in the pasture. I ran to her and leaned against her shoulder and cried out my shame and rage. She kept right on biting at the half-frozen grass. "You don't know there's no feed for you," I told her. "But you've got to have it by hook or by crook."

I left Mabe and hurried to the woods where Laurance was cutting firewood. "Let me help," I said.

"Good. After I trim, you pull the branches away and pile them together. Now that you're here the crosscut'll go better. This two-man saw's hard to work alone." He leaned on his ax and threw sweaty hair off his forehead. His blue eyes crinkled. "Your beans harvested?" he asked.

"Not quite. But I'll finish them later. I want to earn some money." I saw how friendly his eyes were. "Laurance, how come Papa doesn't help us? He sends us whatever he wants to, but when we need something he never gives it."

"I don't know," said Laurance. A shadow of dejection replaced his smile. "You asked him for money for Mabe, didn't you?"

"Yes."

"He said no, of course." He lifted up his ax. Then he put it down and faced me squarely. His mouth spilled hard, bitter words; "Years ago I used to ask him for things. I didn't like the way he treated Mama. I thought he ought to help. And he always said he'd do anything for us kids. But I know now that he meant only if we'd go his way. I asked him for a new suit for eighth-grade graduation and he wrote something about since it was a church school, God would provide. He said I should write to him as a son to a father, not just to ask for things. I haven't written him since."

Laurance had forgotten I was there. He seemed startled when I said, "Me, too. That's what he told me just now, that I shouldn't ask for things."

My brother looked into my downcast face and his expression changed. He grinned. "Shucks! We'll earn our own money. And what we can't have we'll do without." He swung the ax and with one blow severed a four-inch limb. I hauled away the branches and piled them up. With the crosscut we felled big cherry, soft maple and close-grained beech. After a while Laurance said, "That's enough. Let's start cutting."

One at each end of the crosscut we cut the trunks into

sixteen-inch lengths. We let everything lie where it fell till all the trees were in chunks. Then Laurance began to split. With his ax handle he had measured eight feet from a tree and driven in two stakes side by side. "I've made these stakes just four feet high," he said. "When you've piled level with the top of the stakes you'll have a cord. You pile while I split. Bet I can keep ahead of you."

It was almost suppertime. My arms ached. Laurance hurled his blade into a chunk, lifted it with a twist over his shoulder and brought the back of the ax head down with a crack on another block. The heavy chunk of cherry lay parted, showing yellow grain rippled like ribbon candy. When he'd split several chunks I piled them close along the eight-foot space. When it became dark Laurance gave me the ax and shouldered the crosscut. "We've got nearly a cord, besides all that's cut ahead. We earned a good three dollars today—maybe more."

"Mabe and I'll deliver," I said. "If you get me the wagon."

"I'll ask Pete Vanderveldt tomorrow," he said. "He's got a one-horse wagon he doesn't use much. If we can sell enough wood maybe we'll buy a wagon for ourselves, later."

Mr. Vanderveldt was our neighbor on the south. We bought milk from him. He had a beautiful farm, each field rich in crops or grassland. His thirty-year-old mare Daisy looked like a colt. She spent most of her time loafing in deep pasture while he worked with his heavy team.

At noon the next day I went with Laurance. Mr. Vanderveldt was hitching up his team of matched chestnut Percherons. He had a red bandanna around his turtlelike neck. On his pointed head, sandy hair stood straight up. "Vy, you need vagon, you got 'im" His wide mouth grinned amiably. "Take, use like you vant. I need, I ask 'im back."

"Thank you," said Laurance. "We appreciate it."

"No tanks. You velcome. You need udder ting?"

"No, that's all. My sister'll come get the wagon this afternoon."

"Is right dere," said Mr. Vanderveldt. He pointed to a light trim wagon sheltered under a shed. "You no see me, you get." He smiled, eyes blue as cornflowers in his ruddy Dutch face. "Bye bye now." He turned to his work.

In the middle of the afternoon Laurance sent me after the wagon. No one was in the yard so I knocked on the door. Mr. Vanderveldt's sister Nellie came to the door. Her face beamed. "Come in, come in," she said. "You have cake, coffee? Time for snack."

"Hey, you, sit down," called Mr. Vanderveldt from his chair. A red checkered cloth was on the table, which was spread with plates of cake and cookies. He bit off a hunk of chocolate cake and washed it down with coffee. "You come for vagon, no? First, have piece of cake. Cookie?" He waved his hand over the table. "Help yourself."

Timidly I took a chair. I slid a piece of cake onto my plate and took up a fork. Slowly, eyes on my plate, I began to eat.

Laurance rigged side bars on the wagon and while he kept on splitting I piled the first cord on. Mama had already found a customer—Mrs. Bailey in Cleveland, a widow. "She'll be wanting more," said Mama. "Give her good measure, and if she asks you to pile it in her shed, you do it. That's the way to keep customers. You can have half of what you and Laurance earn, for Mabe's keep. But our own firewood has to come first."

Mrs. Bailey looked out through the curtains as I drove into her yard. She came to the woodshed door. "Drive over here," she said. "Back up and throw the wood in the shed." With a hand that trembled she held a shawl around her stooped shoulders. "I'd appreciate it if you'd pile the wood, my rheumatism's so bad."

By the end of November I had bought a ton of hay, fifty pounds of oats and a block of salt for Mabe. She'd need lots more before the winter was over. In spring I'd need seeds and fertilizer, too. There was no end.

Home and School

SPRING came, with pussywillows along the creek and cowslips that shone like gold in the swamp. Mama had an idea. "This summer I'm going to can more than ever." She spoke vigorously as we sat down to breakfast. "I wrote the school principal and he's willing to take canned goods in trade for tuition and board. We'll start right in with cowslip greens and keep on through peaches and pears."

Her cheeks were rosy with excitement as she turned to me. "Laurance has his job on the road. You and I are going to can. I want you to take a burlap bag and go down to the swamp and pick a whole bag of cowslips to get us started. They're in their prime now before the blossoms open up. The leaves are big enough so's you can fill a bag in no time. I'll get the jars ready. I'll work on what you bring while you go back for more."

While Laurance went to work I hurried to the swamp. Under the water the stems were slippery. I sorted out grass, leaves and twigs. Finally the bag was full and I took it to the house. Mama had a wash boiler simmering on the stove. A slew of jars stood on the table. She sat sorting old covers and rubber rings.

When I came in she snatched the bag and took out a bouquet of the marsh marigolds, already wilted from being pressed in the bag. "These are a godsend," she said. "I don't know why I didn't think of them last year. I'll wash these and see how many jars they'll make while you go for more." She emptied the bag into a washtub and handed it back.

For two weeks, while the ground was still partially covered with snow and too wet to work, I gathered cowslips while Mama canned. Some nights were mild and peepers started to sing. On cold nights they were silent. In the morning the cowslips were edged with ice. By the time the stalks had grown tough and the leaves bitter Mama had two hundred jars lined up in the cellar. "Aren't they beautiful!" she exclaimed as she gazed at the glass through which yellow buds winked among dark leaves. "And this is only the beginning. Be sure to plant lots of beans. I'll can them as shell beans, for us and the school. God has sent me this way to earn money so Laurance can go to school this fall."

She climbed the stairs ahead of me and her voice drifted back. "You'll have time to plow and plant before strawberries are ripe. We'll can strawberries, huckleberries and blackberries. If you raise carrots I'll can them while they're young and tender, and then beans before peaches are ripe. Last will be the pears. I'll make applesauce too, though. He said they need some toward spring when apples are scarce."

I tried to share Mama's excitement, but all I could see was work. I brought out my plow and harrow and made sure the work harness was sound. I gave it a good going over with cooking oil on a soaked rag.

My garden was bigger than ever. It included a half acre of beans and enough potatoes to last half the winter. Bluebirds and tree swallows glided overhead. Mabe and I worked to the tune of their warbles and the singing of brown thrashers and songsparrows in the brush. Black snakes escaped before our feet and toads hopped away. As each day brought its own beauty I missed sharing it with Papa. When I drew I longed for his comments, but I was determined not to write to him unless he first wrote me.

One day in September Mama packed the car to take Laurance to school. She jammed hundreds of jars into the back of the Willys, each wrapped in old newspapers. She settled them firmly while I wrapped and handed her jar after jar: golden peaches, cream-white pears, red and purple berries; dark green cowslips and buff-colored beans. I wished I could go to school. I wanted to draw and write, but I didn't know how.

Laurance piled his suitcase and boxes on top of the canned goods. He checked everything, then got behind the wheel. Mama sat next to him, her handbag clutched to her, her lap under a robe. The old touring car sagged in back. "I can feel 'er dragging!" said Laurance as he started the motor. "We'll have to go easy over the bumps."

"Yes, go slow," said Mama. "We'll soon be out to the hard road where it's smooth. Goodbye," she said to me. "Take care of things. I'll be back tomorrow."

The motor coughed and chugged. Laurance shoved in the clutch. "So long, kid," he said gaily. "I'll be seein' you!" He let out the clutch and the car lurched forward and crept out the drive. I watched it move along the muddy ruts, clear to the top of the hill. Then I went to the barn to see Mabe.

Laurance had long ago built her a manger and feed box, and installed thick planks for flooring. The old thrill at owning a real live horse swept over me as I came in the stable. She turned her head and gave a whinny. "You want something," I accused her. "You love me for what you can get." I dipped a scoop of oats and dumped them into her box. She thrust in her nose and began to chew. "You're just like me with Papa," I said. "I always want something. Well, that doesn't mean I don't love him." I stood a long time watching her eat, my hand absently stroking her neck. When she finished the oats she looked around expectantly. "Go on with you," I chided.

I walked to the house and up to my room. As I sat down the picture of that day came back to me clearly—how I'd kicked the table leg in anger and burned the letter so I'd never see it again. The flames hadn't destroyed it, however; I had seen it a thousand times in my mind: "you needn't write again. . . ." My cheeks flushed at the memory. He was right, I was too old for the "gimmes"; but I still needed my father.

From the table drawer I drew out a sheet of paper and took my pen. There in the stillness of the empty house I wrote him a humble note. Not a word about his last letter or even about my horse or the farm work; just nature observations I'd kept pent up too long. I sketched a bluebird at the hole in the apple tree and a bittern I'd seen in the swamp. I signed it "With love," but left out the hugs and kisses. I was too old for that, too. I sent it to the last address he'd given, and ran out to put it in the mail box before I could change my mind.

We got word from Laurance. He was doing well in school. He had a job on the farm afternoons, studied evenings, and at night worked as a watchman. "When does he sleep?" groaned Mama. She wrote him a letter of warning.

Laurance wrote back, "Don't worry, Mama. I fall asleep in the dull classes and sometimes I catch a nap between rounds at night. Guess what? I've made friends with a skunk. At midnight when I sit on the school steps to eat, this skunk comes waddling by and shares my food. The cook packs me a good dinner every evening. I talk with the skunk and he's getting real friendly. He takes food from my hands now."

Once in a while Laurance wrote to me. "Boy, you should see the girls here! Being night watchman's some job. I go through the girls' dorm every night, checking. I'm supposed to announce, 'Man coming,' but I holler low so's not to wake anybody. Sometimes girls are still up giggling in the bathroom and they scurry to their rooms with hardly anything on. Wow!"

Later he told us he sang in the glee club and wrote some for the school paper. His work was a split shift now, driving the milk truck in the morning after his watchman's job, then going directly to class. After classes, dinner and back to the farm, where he worked three hours before knocking off for two hours' sleep before supper. After supper he studied "when I don't go to sleep. But I get most stuff in class and don't need to do much homework."

After Mama wrote bawling him out for overdoing his letters became brief scrawls.

That winter I worked alone with Mabe. I kept our two stoves in wood and now and then got a cord ahead to sell. Mama baked, gave piano lessons and found a few papering jobs. She began to take in washings. I carried water from the creek and she scrubbed the clothes on a washboard. My job was to hang them outdoors, while my hands ached with cold. Some days the sheets hardened into boards before I could get them pinned onto the line.

Mama took care to get the clothes religiously clean. She folded them neatly, and when there was ironing she did a meticulous job. I tried to iron, but after I scorched Mr. Petter's dress shirt she pushed me aside. "Your heart's not in it. I'd rather do it myself."

I spent hours painting greeting cards. Before Christmas I'd made a dozen. I took them first to Vanderveldts. "Iss pretty, no?" exclaimed Miss Vanderveldt, as she spread them on the table so her brother could see. She blinked at me. "You do yourself?"

"Yes."

"Vunderful!"

"How much?" said Mr. Vanderveldt.

"Ten cents apiece."

"Vy, not bad," said Miss Vanderveldt. "Handmade like dis. Ve take two, eh, Peter?"

She picked two sunset scenes with church spires silhouetted against dark trees. When she paid me I made for the door. My heart pounded. I've actually sold two pictures, I thought. If I sold ten more I'd have $1.20, earned by drawing.

"Humph," said Mama when I told her. "Who's going to buy pictures? Most people can't afford food and fuel."

I tried at a few houses in town. "Pretty," they said. "But we can't afford handmade cards. They're two for a nickel at the store." I brought the cards home and sent them to relatives.

"Don't fret," said Mama. "You can earn more cutting wood. And you're making money when you hang out the clothes and carry water so I can get the washings done."

"But I like to draw. I've got my first money as an artist."

"Twenty cents! That won't go far." She sorted a batch of dirty clothes into piles. "You're your father all over again. Now start carrying water. I'll need a lot to get these work clothes clean."

As I skipped down the hill to the creek I chanted, "I'm an artist. I've sold two pictures."

A week before Christmas a flat package came from Papa. Pasted to it was a letter, the first one I'd received since my olive-branch note in September. I ripped open the envelope and found two pages in his hasty scrawl. After apologizing for the delay ("Your letter just reached me, forwarded from my old address") he wrote as he always had, commenting first on my sketches. He said my style had improved. He went on to tell me about birds he'd seen lately and work he'd had published and paintings he'd been commissioned to do.

"Attached is a pad of fine drawing paper, tubes of watercolor and a set of brushes. The brushes are old, but better than new ones you'd buy there. I've got an idea. How about me giving you drawing lessons by mail? I'd give you regular assignments; you'd send your work to me for criticism; then I'd return it for you to study."

Wow! I wrote back and waited for the first lesson. He sent me assignments every two weeks, which taught me elementary rules of light and shade, perspective and composition. It took me hours to get each one ready. I was never satisfied. Neither was he. He praised my efforts, but he always told how I could do better. He insisted that beautiful colors were wasted on a poorly done drawing. He said my best picture would always be my next.

When spring came I put aside my drawing and planned a bigger garden than ever. We'd gotten through the winter, but Mabe's heaves were worse. I wanted another horse. "I need a team, Mama. Pulling that plow's too much for Mabe. With another horse I could plow more of our land and I'd hire out with my team."

"Yes, and have another mouth to feed. You'd have to buy double harness and different tools. Why aren't you satisfied with what you've got?" It was a chill April evening. She sat with the mending basket in her lap. "Here, if you want more to do. Darn one of your socks. How you do wear holes!"

Reluctantly I threaded a needle. In and out with tiresome monotony the needle traveled, going nowhere. My feet fidgeted as they never did when I was drawing.

By this time I had fenced all our farm but the woodland, by running wires from tree to tree. Mabe roamed over much of our seventy acres, but except for the close-cropped grass in the yard and around the barn the only grass was poverty grass—barbed tussocks spaced among moss and stones. Mabe pruned blackberry bushes and maples and even wild cherry as well as the scrub apples back on the hill. When she worked I gave her hay and a few oats. She had never been fat, but now she looked gaunt.

That April I picked only enough cowslips for our own use. "The school doesn't want them," said Mama. "The students left them on their plates. But they'll use all the berries and fruit I can muster. And more shell beans than before." When school was out she drove the Willys to bring Laurance home and collect the empty jars to use again. Laurance arrived at the wheel of the car, cap at a jaunty angle. "Hi, kid," he yelled before the motor stopped. "Make way to the food!" His blue eyes shone from deep in their sockets. Over one eyebrow dangled a lock of tousled hair. His face had the old grin. But his cheeks were hollow. He was thinner than I'd ever seen him.

He leaped out of the car, slammed the door and charged into the kitchen. "Food!" he called. He wrenched off the cover to the bread can, broke off a hunk of bread and stuffed it into his mouth. The rest of the loaf he took to the table, after grabbing a soup dish from the cupboard and detouring to the pantry for a pitcher of milk. As he crumbed the bread in great chunks and swashed milk over it, I handed him a spoon. "Man, I'm starving," he cried and began to eat. "Is there any fruit?" he asked around a mouthful.

I ran down cellar and brought up a can of huckleberries. He poured half a quart over his bread. "M-m-m-m," his voice came in muffled contentment. "Man, this is nourishment."

Mama staggered in with a box of jars.

"Leave all that stuff," Laurance said. "Let me eat and I'll bring everything in."

"All right," said Mama. She set the box near the pantry and sat down to get her breath. "My, you're thin, Laurance. I noticed that right away. You should've eaten more."

"Eat? Eat when this stuff they pay you a quarter for, they serve in dinky helpings at five cents each? Why, they get over a dollar for a jar of these berries."

"Well, they've got to make a profit."

"If I'd eaten all I wanted I wouldn't have lasted long," said Laurance. "I left owing money."

"We'll try to make it up this summer," said Mama. "I checked with your road boss and he's saved a place for you on the job. He's promised you a raise, too."

"I'll start tomorrow," said Laurance. He sat back from the table. "Man, that was good. They've got a bakery at school but they don't make bread like yours. I only took two slices to a meal, too, it cost so much. Most of the time I only ate two meals a day."

"I'll fatten you up," said Mama. "I'll make a batch of doughnuts tomorrow and some apple pies. They'll go good in your dinner pail."

"Boy, will they!" He scanned the crumbs on the table, the empty bowl and half jar of fruit. "I could eat another loaf," he said. "But it'd kill me." He rose. "You open the door for me, kid, while I bring in the things."

For his road job, Laurance left before daylight and came home late for supper. His face became bronzed from sun and the fumes of hot tar, his hands black and calloused. On days when rain poured down, he fixed things around the house, carried water for Mama and tinkered with his three-wheeler. He had started an airplane, too, and spent hours with a drawshave shaping two-by-fours into struts. On some rainy days and Sundays he took the Willys to visit dumps and came home with bolts, nuts, bits of wire and pieces of metal. He found Model-T wheels that would do for the three-wheeler and a set of old motorcycle wheels for the plane's landing gear. He kept everything spread on the barn floor.

When my plow broke he put in a new point. He showed me how to rivet a broken harness. For Mama he devised a pulley so we could handle the drying without stepping into mud or snow.

Meanwhile, Mabe and I raised vegetables. I still couldn't buy fertilizer, but I spread her manure as far as it would go. When strawberries were ripe I picked at Mr. Rosen's for one cent a quart. He had two acres and hired a gang of pickers. We took a tray of empty quarts and a stack of extras and ran for the first rows. Most of the pickers were women and girls, but there were some boys. The big boys scared me. In my hand-me-down overalls, with long straight hair and timid manner I was fair game. They soon found that I blushed furiously when they teased me. "Come on in the woods, I'll show you something," said one fellow. He snapped his suspenders, and winked at the rest of his bunch. They guffawed. Blood rushed to my face.

"Oh, she knows how to blush," he went on. "I wonder what else she knows." Amid cries of "Rube" and "Hayseed" they pelted me with berries. They moved off as a couple of housewives came down the next row. I tried to keep near other women, where the pack could not prey upon me.

One day at quitting time an older guy who had a Buick

said, "Want a ride home?" I knew what might happen if a girl accepted a ride. As I hesitated, my tormentors assembled and whispered together, glancing my way. In terror of them, I hopped in the car.

"How was the picking?" he said as we roared off in a jackrabbit start.

"All right. How'd you do?"

"Not bad." Silence. The motor hummed. My hair blew into my mouth. I couldn't think of a thing to say. I'd never ridden alone with a boy before. Without seeming to look, I saw his hawklike face with stiff black hair like a roached mane above a pimply brow. His mouth had a quirk at the corner.

"Ever see a one-hand driver?" he asked. With a lazy motion he took one hand off the wheel and laid it over the seat above my shoulders. Then he let it drop, gauging my reaction, like a horseman gentling a skittish colt. At his touch all Mama's training leaped up. "Stop!" I screamed, and flung his arm from me. "Let me out or I'll jump."

"Well, all right," he said with scorn. "Keep your pants on." He braked with a jolt. Before the car stopped I had swung open the door and jumped out. I slammed the door and scooted down the road. As I ran I could hear his laughter. "Nobody'll ever kiss *you*!" he shouted. He turned and backed in a flurry of gravel, and sped away.

I ran to the barn so Mama wouldn't see me until I had recovered. I didn't let on what had happened. Huckleberries had started to ripen. I told her I wasn't going back to the strawberry field, but would begin to pick huckleberries instead. She was going to pick too.

Stella and Chub

MAMA dressed for berrying in a fresh, clean housedress, low in the neck over her ample bosom. Heavy cotton stockings protected her legs. Her thick dark hair, firmly pinned into a high bun, had enough wave to hold all day, only damp ringlets escaping, which she reached to tuck into place.

We picked for George Stanley down near Cleveland. He had acres and acres of wild bushes loaded with fruit. We started out before daylight, to pick as soon as we could see. Mama picked for canning and pies. I picked for cash. He paid three cents a quart. On days when Mama baked to sell I rode down on Mabe.

Mr. Stanley's hobby was horse-trading. When the huckleberry season started he was driving two black horses. One was Stella, a big lame mare. One day when I rode into the yard he was hitching a new horse into the wagon with Stella. The new one was a close-coupled little gelding, burnished copper with creamy white mane and tail. His face was lighted by a crooked blaze. His short body, dainty ears and small feet made the rangy Stella look grotesque. He was like a flowering peach tree I'd found once in the dump—pure beauty against an ugly background.

I tied Mabe under a tree and walked over to watch Mr. Stanley hitch up. He was a hard-faced man and I didn't like the way he handled horses. "Back up!" he yelled, and when they failed to move quick enough he strode to their heads and sawed on the bits, skewing the horses' mouths and making their tongues bulge out. Stella backed awkwardly, her right hind foot flying up. She was afflicted with stringhalt.

"What's his name?" I asked.

"Chub," he said. He linked a trace to the whiffle-tree.

"Where'd he come from?"

"Got him in a trade—my other black with something to boot."

"Isn't he too small to go with Stella?"

"Oh, I may trade Stella off. Or if I sell Chub, I might get a bigger horse."

"You mean you'd sell Chub?" My heart began a high-wire act.

"Sure. Sell anything on four feet." He darted me a keen look. "Why? You want him?"

"How much you asking?"

"Eighty dollars. He's sound. Not broke single, but you could train him in a wink. Look how he's built. He's an easy keeper."

I watched Mr. Stanley put his heavy foot on the hub, swing up to the wagon and carelessly gather the lines. "Think it over," he said and drove off. Chub's feet stepped pertly, trying to keep up with Stella's awkward gait.

After that I entered the Stanley yard every day with the fear that Chub would be gone. When I saw him still there, ears alert, feet nimble, I said a prayer of thanks. He had a pale mane and tail flowing like rich cream, and his red-gold coat was frosted with silver. He wore white stockings on his hind legs.

I asked Mr. Stanley if he could be ridden.

"Never has been, but I don't see why not."

I began to scheme. We got paid daily for what we picked, and each night I took out the cigar box in which I kept my money and added the day's earnings, counting the whole thing over again. When picking was good I made as high as three dollars a day. I'd been saving for Mabe's winter feed plus a nest-egg for school. Mama'd said maybe in another year I could go. After seeing Chub I didn't worry about school. I wanted him more than I'd ever wanted anything.

I forced my fingers to move faster. I gulped down my noon sandwich and went right back to pick instead of taking a rest. One night when Mama was getting ready for bed I brought up the subject of Chub. "I'm sorry," she said. "I haven't got the money." She went on braiding her hair, the long thick pigtail different from the firm no-nonsense bun of the day. I looked for a weak spot.

"He'd pay for himself," I pleaded. "With a team I could find more work."

"Pshaw!" She held the end of her long braid with one hand while she fumbled on the dresser for a rubber band. "Mabe doesn't pay for her keep as it is. We can't afford another horse." She snapped the rubber around her hair and turned to her bed. The mattress sagged under her weight and the rusty springs creaked.

"But, Mama, eighty dollars is cheap, and I've got all my berry money."

"Well, if you want him, you'll have to buy him yourself. I've got the mortgage and the taxes and we've got to eat. And Laurance has to go to school." For a moment she sat on the edge of the bed with closed eyes. She opened them again. "How much berry money've you got?" she asked.

"More than forty dollars. That's over half, and I can maybe get five dollars more before berrying's done. Won't that do, Mama? Can't you give me the rest?"

"No, I can't," she said. "Why, that's a fortune." She lifted her legs into the bed, laid her head on the pillow with a sigh and pulled up the sheet. "Now turn out the light and go to bed."

I turned down the wick and blew out the light. The dying flame sent hot fumes upward to sting my nostrils.

"I'm sorry," murmured Mama. "Goodnight, dear."

I felt my way through the darkness and threw myself onto my bed. Tears wouldn't help. My mind stacked the berry money and figured the price of beans. Dry beans sold for five cents a pound and I'd have a lot once they got ripe.

Even the beans wouldn't be enough, though, and Chub would be sold long before harvest. I thought of Mama's favorite saying, "What can't be cured must be endured." The only thing left was Stella. I could still have my team.

In the morning I told Mr. Stanley I'd buy Stella.

"I thought you wanted the little one," he said, searching my face.

"I can't afford Chub," I said. "I've just got forty dollars. Stella'll make me a team." I made myself look at Stella's black hammer head on her long neck.

"You sure, now?" Mr. Stanley asked as he studied my face. "Couldn't your mother chip in?"

"No, she couldn't," I snapped.

"All right. I've got a job to do today, but you can take her back with you tonight."

From my pocket I brought the folded bills and quarters and dimes and nickels and counted them into his hand. His thumb closed possessively over each bill as it landed and he cupped his other hand for the change. "There!" I said. I grabbed my pail and withdrew to the shelter of the field.

"I'll be in early," he called after me. "Don't worry, you'll have her tonight."

I didn't want her. I wanted Chub. But she was a horse and I needed a team. As I led her home that evening I looked back at her long neck. Her halt foot leaped up with each step, to strike the ground with a jolt. I tied her in the stall and started to curry her. When I rubbed the comb down over her right hind leg her foot sprang up with a jerk.

Mama gave me a cheerful look when I came in to supper. She had been out with baked goods and just got back. "Set the table," she said. "Run down cellar and get the beans and potatoes. If there's any lettuce left in the garden pick some of that."

I stumped listlessly down cellar and back. Mama gave me a sharp look. "Did you get your horse today? You said you were going to buy the black."

"Yes, I got her."

As I started out to pick lettuce Mama's voice pinned

me. "Aren't you glad? Now you've got your team."

"Yeah, I'm happy." I said the mammoth lie crossly. I let the screen door slam and went out to the lettuce, where a few leaves lingered, curled and seared with heat.

A week later huckleberries were over. For the first time I had a chance to hitch up my team. Chub was still at Stanley's, teamed now with a rangy bay called Ruby, bigger and more raw-boned than Mabe. "Picked her up cheap," Mr. Stanley gloated. "I'm holding out on Chub. Guy offered me sixty but I wouldn't take it. He's worth eighty if he's worth a dime."

The next morning I went out to plow. I'd picked up a double harness and two-horse plow secondhand with a doubletree thrown in. Stella, like Mabe, stood quietly while I harnessed her. I brought them out of the barn and hitched them together. I began to plow with my gawky team. As Stella's foot flew helplessly up and came stamping down I grew more and more miserable. I'd paid forty dollars to witness agony. Her limbs moved like scarecrow sticks. Her eyes had a haggard look. Of course she could never be ridden. I couldn't even use her to plow, for after a couple hours I knew that I couldn't bear the sight. I unhitched the team and drove back to the barn before noon. After they'd cooled off I let them out to pasture. I walked on past them, a pail in my hand, to look for blackberries.

While my hands dodged briars I built up a daring scheme, stacking it block on block like a child's tower. Only the shiftless bought things on time. Yet Mama owed a mortgage and paid it in installments. She never knew where the money would come from. It came, though, because she worked for it and saved for it. I decided to ask Mr. Stanley if he'd take back Stella and let me have Chub. I'd pay the difference at five dollars a month.

Early the next morning I jumped on Mabe and started for Stanleys'. *What if Chub was already gone*! "Hurry up, Mabe," I said and dug my heels into her ribs. When I got there Mr. Stanley's gray head moved from behind the partition beyond which I saw the whisk of a cream-colored tail. "I just fed Chub his oats," he said. He threw the scoop in the bin and made the hasp tight. "Everything all right?" he asked as I stood speechless.

"I came to see if I could buy Chub," I blurted. "Trade Stella and pay the boot at five dollars a month."

Chub's hooves stirred the straw. His teeth chomped the grain. In a dark corner a pitchfork caught a glint of sun on its triple tines. Mr. Stanley's seamed face wore its usual expression of cynicism. "How'll you get the money?" he asked.

"I've got my beans yet. I'll work in the woods this winter. He should be paid for by spring."

"You know you'll have to give me a paper, and I have the right to take him back any time you don't pay? You know that, don't you?" His barbed eyes snagged me like fishhooks.

"Y-yes."

"All right. It's a deal. I'm working Chub today, but I'll bring him out to your place tomorrow and get Stella. I've got some business out your way. Wait here a minute. I'll go in and get the paper and we'll make out the bargain right now."

When he'd gone to the house I looked in on Chub. "Whoa, boy," I said. He stepped right over. I walked in beside him, to stand close to his head and watch him chew, oats dribbling from his lips. His small neat ears flickered. When I reached out my hand to smooth his neck, quick as lightning, he turned and bit me savagely in the chest.

Mr. Stanley's granite face shuddered when I told him. "Never stand beside a horse while he's eating," he said. "Not unless you know the horse. You still want him?"

"Sure." We made out the paper. Chub was mine.

Next morning Mr. Stanley's lumber wagon rattled into our drive. Chub's short legs pumped to keep up with Ruby's long strides. I led Stella out. Mr. Stanley dragged the harness off Chub and put on a much-mended halter. "There's your horse," he said as he handed me the tie rope. "You'd better take him to the barn."

Chub followed willingly, his breath warm at my elbow. He picked up his feet the moment he laid them down. I tied him next to Mabe, then rushed out to Mr. Stanley. He backed Stella in, fastened her traces and snapped her yoke to the pole. Taking up the lines he vaulted into the high seat. "So long," he called, slapped the lines, and the team trotted out the driveway, Stella's leg rising and falling like the handle of a pump.

I hitched up my new team and drove to the field where the plow waited. Chub danced along, shaking his head and snorting. At the plow I adjusted the lines around my waist, gripped the handles and clucked to my team. Chub charged ahead while Mabe was still leaning into her collar. His head tossed, his feet stamped. The plow point dug in, and a smooth roll of earth folded over the share. Suddenly the point struck a root. Chub stopped, reared and began to back rapidly right over his singletree.

"Whoa!" I rushed to stop him before he could tangle with the plow beam, and led him even with Mabe, who stood stolidly in the furrow. Starting again, I called, "Come on!" Chub lunged before Mabe could get underway, then snapped back as though pulled by a rubber band. As I tried again and again to make him pull, words of Grandma's dinned themselves into me. "Handsome is as handsome does." With dismay I surveyed Chub's flowing mane and tail, burnished copper coat and boundless vigor. He was so handsome. I unhitched and drove back to the barn. Chub's ears pricked forward and he broke into a trot. Every time he felt the lines tighten he tossed his head and snorted and threatened to back.

I put on the single harness and hitched him to the buggy. Down the dirt trail to the creek we went, splashing through the creek and up the far side. He was a ticking bomb. Half way up through the pasture he stopped short, ears twitching, then started backing swiftly down the hill. The front wheels cramped and the buggy tipped. I jumped out and grabbed his bridle, led him to straighten out the wheels, and tried again. This time he kept on up the hill, mincing like a parade horse. At the far end of the pasture he reared on his hind feet, whirled, almost upsetting the buggy, and made a race for home. Each time I tried to slow him down, he snorted and shook his head. We careened down the hill, splattered madly through the creek and bounced up to the barn. "Whoa!" He stopped at the stable door, so short that I hit the dashboard.

The next morning, confronted with Chub's doings, Mr. Stanley glowered. "Chub's not balky. You knew he was high-strung. I thought that's why you wanted him."

"But I can't work him."

"Always worked fine for me." He was about to start out with Ruby and Stella, a plow piled on top of a harrow in his wagon. "I'll come by tomorrow and show you a thing or two. You just don't handle him right."

The following day Mr. Stanley came. At the field he threw the lines around his waist, gripped the plow handles and yelled, "Giddap!" The horses started, the plow scraped in. The point found a hidden root. Mabe settled down to pull. Chub jigged and began to back. "Get the blankety-blank out of there!" yelled Mr. Stanley in a roar that could be heard half a mile. Startled, Chub threw himself into his collar, dug in his toenails and pulled. The two horses strained, feet fighting the ground. The root snapped apart, letting the plow through, and a ribbon of fresh earth rolled out. Twice they went around the field. Chub danced at the end of each furrow, tossed his head, and when the going got rough shook his mane and snorted, but he didn't stop. Each time, before he could do so, Mr. Stanley let out a roar. At the third round he said, "You try it."

I settled the lines and said, "Come on!" Mabe started. Chub flew back. "Get out of here!" I screeched, mimicking Mr. Stanley. Chub buckled down. We began to plow. Whenever the plow hit a root I gave a yell.

"All right?" said Mr. Stanley as I stopped beside him. "Bawl the blazes out of 'em so they'll know who's boss. Let a horse have his own way, you'll spoil him. If he does stop on you, holler 'Whoa!' then go up and fiddle with the harness or lift a foot and tap it. He'll forget it was his notion to stop."

Day by day I worked with the team. We plowed and harrowed, pulled stumps and hauled stones. I decided to try riding him, and with only the bridle on I led him next to the rails of the gate. I climbed to the top rail, held the lines clutched together with a clump of mane and crouched for a moment. What would happen? I looked at the rock-strewn ground and the stone barn ramp. One of Chub's ears pointed forward, another back, as he edged skittishly away from the rails. I eased onto his back and tightened my legs against his sides. "Whoa, boy." He gave a violent shudder. His ears turned back to listen. Then he swiveled his head and stared at me there on his back. When I said, "Come on, Chub," he began to amble, then to trot. He broke into a canter, smooth as a rockinghorse. His mouth answered each tug of the reins as we wheeled around under the maples, down past the barn and up the other side. "Whoa!" I said. He braked in mid-stride. I went flying over his head to land in a tangle of rocks and blackberries.

The road past our house was too stony and filled with ruts for a fast pace, but a mile up the road on a deserted farm lay a quarter-mile stretch of smooth, solid dirt. I rode Chub up there whenever I could. At the start I bent to his ear and whispered, "S-s-s-t," our signal for speed. He leaped into a canter and went pounding up the track, one ear forward, the other back. At the end, where the path abruptly disappeared in a tangle of brush, he spun around, lifting both forefeet, and tore down the stretch, headed for home.

Pines and Wheat

ONE AUGUST evening I heard Mama and Laurance talking. At breakfast Mama announced the winter's plan. "Laurance isn't going back to school this year," she said. "I'll take the canned goods to apply on next year's tuition and he'll work here this winter to get ahead." She speared a slice of toast and brought it to her. "We're going to cut the pines."

Laurance's face was a rock.

I opened my mouth. "But, Mama—"

"Don't say a word," she said as she munched her toast. "I know how you feel about the pines. But they've got to go. Otherwise we'll lose the farm. And Laurance *must* go to school."

"Isn't there some other way? I'll work with Chub."

"Pshaw! It'll take you months to pay for him and you've still got to feed him. The pines are prime. We've got to be practical, dear." She crammed another piece of toast into her mouth.

"But they've been there hundreds of years."

"Then it's time. It's a waste to let them stand longer."

Laurance sat silent, his face turned from me. I got up and fled to the woods. At the base of a giant pine I sank into thick needles. Far above, branches made a rushing sound like a waterfall. Mama's just like Grandpa, I thought. She's going to destroy these like he did her lilacs.

The breeze from the pine tops stooped to brush my cheek. I leaned against the bark and looked along the aisle of pines, each tree a giant. After awhile I got to my feet and strode back to the house. A month later Laurance got the crosscut set and sharpened and had me turn the grindstone while he put an edge on the axes. Our job was to fell all the prime timber, cut it in lengths and haul the logs to the sawmill. Laurance and I would spend the winter alone. Mama had gotten work as a housekeeper for a rich household fifty miles away.

November came. A brisk wind tossed the manes of the horses as they plunged down the trail to the woods. I tied the team to a tree and Laurance shouldered the crosscut. A roar reached us from branches threshed by the wind. Laurance gazed upward along the bole of a towering pine. "With this wind we may have trouble."

Laurance's ax struck into the first pine. He swung again and again, till a yellow gash yawned across the side where he wanted the tree to fall. He set the ax aside and picked up the saw. "Take one end," he said. "Get a move on."

I knelt in the pine duff and held up my end of the six-foot saw. "Hold the blade higher," he snapped. "We've got to get above the notch," and as I scrambled to my feet to hold it up, "Hey, not too high. Keep it straight, can't you?" Back and forth the saw moved in two-foot strokes until the jagged teeth held, then as we grasped the handles in both hands and spread our feet, bending low, the blade whipped to and fro in three-foot strokes. "Hey, don't curve it. Just pull, don't push. You're making a belt out of the blade," Laurance scolded.

The teeth automatically cleared themselves of chips as they swept through with a z-z-z-z-t, z-z-z-z-t, causing fragrant sawdust to pour out the scent of pine. Z-z-z-z-t, z-z-z-z-t. "Wait, Laurance, I'm tired." I straightened up, my fingers still curled from holding the handle. We bent again. As the cut deepened the swaying branches brought pressure that made the saw bind. Laurance pulled a steel wedge from his pocket and drove it into the cut. We sawed some more. As the wedge joggled at a strong gust Laurance said, "Be ready. If I yell 'Timber!' let go and run—back toward the team."

After a few more strokes there came a creak and the cut widened. "Timber!" shrieked Laurance. He jerked out the saw. With a heavy groan the tree toppled. A sigh whispered in its massive crown. As it gained momentum it moved faster; the last fibers splintered at the base and the crown whipped downward, throwing the butt off the stump to tunnel deep in the duff. The crown did not reach the ground, however. It made a twist, crashed into the top of a maple and came to rest there—lodged.

Now, where the great crown had been yawned unaccustomed light. The surrounding trees seemed trying to draw a tattered curtain over the space.

"We're in a mess," said Laurance. He scratched his ear. "I can fix it, though." Coiling a rope over his shoulder he took the ax and climbed the leaning pine trunk. About twenty feet up he stopped and shook out the rope. "I'll fasten one end here," he called. "You hitch the team to that end and head'em over between those hemlocks. Don't let'em move till I tell you."

"What'll you do?" I asked.

"I'm going to chop it nearly through and as soon as I hear—or feel—a crack, you'll pull it away, letting the crown fall. Meanwhile I'll be around behind this maple in case I need to chop again."

By the time the team stood ready near the hemlocks Laurance had made a wide V in the pine. At each blow the trunk jarred, but it made no sound. Then, without warning, it snapped. The bottom part fell from under Laurance before he could grab the maple. With a yell he dropped with it, while the ponderous crown jackknifed in slow-motion, and with a swish and a thud crashed down right on him. Branches snapped like pretzels; broken pieces were hurled helter-skelter.

"Whoa!" I commanded as I threw down the lines and ran to kneel by the welter of branches. There was a stir and a branch quivered. Laurance groaned. "I can't move," he said. "Get the ax and cut some of these branches. Watch out you don't cut *me*."

When I'd taken away a few branches I found him lying on his back, two stubs and the log itself like a wicket over him.

"Go get two-by-fours and crib it up," he said calmly. He saw my face and forced a lopsided grin. "Only my hip's hurt a little. It's nothing."

I unhitched Chub and galloped toward the barn. We were soon headed back with a bunch of old timbers bumping behind. "Shove one under at an angle," said Laurance. "Cross another over and so on till they're up tight under the log. Do that at each end of me, then cut these stubs. I can wiggle out if the trunk doesn't settle."

Half an hour later he had wormed his way out and stood up, supported with a caneline stick. In two weeks he limped back to the woods and we went on with the job.

Deep into the stand we worked our way. I stacked brush and lengthened skid trails. Chub was a good skid horse. He could turn on a dime, and his enthusiasm as he jittered along, chain catching on roots to make him bound with impatience, kept the work lively. His hooves cut crescents in the snow as he got a log going, and as it bumped along the path, whipping around curves, I held onto the lines and squeezed past saplings, jumped stumps and dodged branches. A chickadee flitted above me shouting, "Dee-dee-dee!" at the moment a snow-laden bough hit me whap! in the face.

Day after day we skidded out logs and loaded them on the bobsled. I delivered them while Laurance kept cutting. It was during a blizzard when we couldn't work in the woods that Laurance conceived another invention. "How'd you like a little sleigh you could drive Chub in, floating right over the drifts?" He gazed out the front window at whirling snow.

"Really!"

"I've got an old pair of skis. Found 'em in the dump. I was going to use 'em for winter landing-gear on my plane, but that's a long way off." He grabbed a pencil and began sketching. "Here's how it'll look." In a few minutes he had a diagram. "I'll use strap iron for strength without weight. The seat'll be just high enough to clear drifts, but you'll still have that low-down feeling, close to the horse. I'll offset the thills so the horse'll travel in the left-hand track."

He bundled up and hurried out to the barn to collect materials. For the next three days the kitchen was his workshop as he ripped lumber into strips, shaped them with drawshave and knife, heated metal in the fire to bend it, drilled holes and fastened bolts. "I won't put the thills on in here," he said, "or we couldn't get it out the door. But I'll get 'em ready."

Finally the dainty ski-sled stood complete, topped by a seat made of curved metal and upholstered in red leatherette studded all around with brass-headed tacks. The metalwork was shiny black, and so were the skis and thills. The storm was over and the road had been opened by passing teams. It was 10° below zero. As I led Chub from the stable his hair stood on end. "I'll take him first," said Laurance. "He's frisky and I don't want to wreck it right off."

Laurance jumped into the seat and gripped the lines. "Let 'er go!" he shouted and I released the bridle. Chub bounded through the snow, out the driveway and up the road, with Laurance, perched on the spidery ski-sled skimming behind. I slapped my arms and hopped around to keep warm until they came tearing back. "Light as a feather," Laurance said. "And it didn't give an inch. Here, hold him a minute." He got down and examined the struts. "Solid," he said.

I climbed to the smooth red seat. Laurance let go the bridle and Chub took off up the road. There was no dashboard. His hooves moved under my nose and his tail whipped my face. Later, when I tried to thank Laurance he laughed. "It was nothing. Just a little toy I dreamed up. My airplane's going to be a mite harder."

After Mama had left, we lived at first on shredded wheat and oatmeal and pancakes for breakfast, with a jar of fruit or an apple now and then. For dinner we had hearty sandwiches of baked beans or peanut butter; for supper, beans, potatoes and cowslip greens or carrots. Every other day I got milk from Mr. Vanderveldt.

As winter wore on, however, our supplies ran low. Margarine had long ago vanished. The cowslips and carrots were gone. There were only a few more apples and a dozen jars of fruit. One morning I brought up the last of the potatoes.

"I've got four dollars," Laurance said. "Mama may not send more for a month. Now, we've got to get some kind of food that'll give most strength for least dough."

"Shredded wheat?"

"No, too expensive. So are pancakes or anything else fancy."

"Flour, so I can make bread?"

"That's more like it." He balanced a mound of corn-meal mush on his spoon. "But I know something better. I know what we can get that will be cheaper than flour and we can use it for three meals a day." He plopped the mush into his mouth. "What's the perfect food?" he asked, and before I could answer he said, "Wheat! You know those whole kernels they feed chickens? You can buy a big bag for less than four bucks and I'll bet it would last the rest of the winter. We'd have a little left over for milk to go with it and we'd pour sauce on like we do with shredded wheat."

"There's not much sauce left."

"All right. We'll just eat wheat. They say it's the perfect food."

On my way home from the mill that day I got a hundred-pound bag of chicken feed. Laurance dragged it into the kitchen. "There's our grub," he said.

Two weeks later our fruit was gone. No more money for milk. Nothing but wheat. I began to get a sick feeling every time I dipped into the kettle to dish up mushy gray kernels, split open with pasty insides. Nevertheless, I put a panful on the range each morning. One day while manning the crosscut Laurance sank in the snow. "I'm weak," he said. "My legs feel like putty."

"Same here," I said. It had been growing harder and harder to pick up my feet, and everything seemed too heavy to lift. "What's the matter with us?"

"It's the wheat. I can hardly eat it anymore," he said.

"May I write to Mama?"

"No. If she had money she'd have sent it. She'd only worry."

"Why can't we live on wheat?" I said. "Chickens do."

"We're spoiled. We go too much by taste." He hoisted himself out of the snow. "One thing's sure, we're not going to beg. Let's get to work."

Beside my bed that night I prayed for food. The mail brought nothing except a letter from Papa asking why I'd neglected my last drawing lesson. I read it to Laurance and we laughed together. "Send him a picture of wheat," he said. "Golden grain waving in a field."

Laurance's irrepressible spirit kept us stubbornly on. One day Mama sent a letter with a ten-dollar bill folded inside. I stocked up on beans, potatoes and cornmeal and bought a whole bushel of apples. There was money enough for a bag of flour, and yeast and shortening for bread. I went to Vanderveldts' for milk again. More than half of the wheat was still in the bag. Laurance took it out to the stable and we fed it to the horses to eke out their oats.

Sandy

MAMA came home in spring. She got paid for the lumber, squared her most pressing debts and put some aside for school. She bought a Jersey cow named Babe and I got a yellow cat called Gretel. The cat slept in the cow's manger. Mama resumed her canning, baking, paper-hanging, washing and piano lessons while I learned to milk the cow and cleared land for more crops. Laurance worked on the road. On rainy days and Sundays he fixed up the stable with concrete floor and a stanchion for the cow.

The cow was due to freshen and I told Mama I was going to be with her when she did. I'd never seen a calf born. The bull had been a Holstein and I hoped the calf wouldn't take after him. I wanted a brown Jersey just like the mother, and I prayed for a heifer calf. I'd raise her. I'd sell milk and butter and she'd be all mine, right from birth.

I went in beside Babe and laid my hand on her paunch. It was pushed out more on one side than the other and stretched so high that her hip bones scarcely showed. Her rib cage moved in and out. I pressed my ear against her flank. I smelled the milky fragrance of her udder, which was already distended. Something hit my cheek like a gloved fist. "Hey, you're alive." I spoke to my calf through the cow's side. "Alive and kicking." Babe swung her head around with a "Moo." I didn't know whether she was talking to me or the calf.

After she had eaten I let her out to nibble the April grass. She stayed out all day. That evening she didn't show up at the barn. I gazed up the hill to the pasture, where the sun cast shadows of the wild cherries. Nothing moved among them. I recalled Grandpa saying, "They'll sneak away if you don't watch out. Hide from you slick as a whistle."

In the barn I had a birthing place all ready behind the horses. It was lined with straw and had a gate through which I would lead Babe when she was about to drop her calf. I wouldn't tie her, but let her move around as she pleased.

In the pasture, Babe's tracks were everywhere in soft dirt, among the dry tussocks of grass. I ran from one blackberry-laced thicket to another, and called her name. No answer. Darkness fell. I felt lost and alone up there in the brushy pasture. Was Babe hiding in that dense clump of trees? I moved toward them, calling, and was startled to hear a low, excited moo. I could hear her move restlessly behind a wall of blackberries that reached in among the trees. A sharp cane ripped my face; prickers tore my hands as I forced my way through and found her under a spreading beech, protected on all sides by briars. As I crept forward she backed away, head down, and gave a bellow. She jerked her head and stamped her foot.

"So, Babe. S-o-o-o, boss. It's only me." Slowly I edged behind her and urged her out. She pressed through the tunnel of thorns, hesitated a moment, looked wildly around, then galloped heavily down the hill.

She was reluctant to enter the new pen, balked at the gate and sniffed the straw. I brought her a pail of water and she drank. I lit the lantern and hung it so it would shine directly into the pen. Babe paced nervously. She glanced back and bit her flank like biting a fly. The calf would surely come soon. I could hardly wait.

I remembered Mama and supper and other humdrum things. I'd need a blanket to stay out all night, and shears to cut the cord and iodine from the medicine chest.

"So you think she'll calve soon," said Mama. "You'd better get right to bed in case you have to get up in the night."

"I'm going to sleep in the barn."

"What if she doesn't have her calf tonight?"

"I'm sure it's tonight. Her bag's full, and she moos as if something hurts."

"All right, go on out there. But wrap up warm. Make sure the lantern's hung right so it won't catch the barn afire."

Mama let me have the shears and iodine. She reminded me to take a pillow and a blanket. I filled my plate with supper and took it to the barn. When I got there Babe was crouched on her knees, and as I reached the gate she sprang up and wheeled with a loud bawl. She tramped round and round the enclosure. She stopped. A flood of liquid gushed out into the straw. She lay down hastily and I saw something pale emerge, the front legs of the calf, folded tight together, enveloped in a sack thin as tracing paper. On top of the legs, nose straight ahead, lay the calf's head.

The cow strained and looked around. Now and then she gave a deep moan. I hoped Mama wouldn't hear. I wanted to be alone with my cow and calf. Babe was trying hard to expel the calf and I wished I could help. But she didn't need me. The calf's body slipped out, done up in transparent film and trailing blood. Babe got up and turned to her bull calf, where he lay moving feebly inside the membrane. She licked him in long strokes. Her sandpaper tongue slapped him around and sloughed off the birth covering. She licked right across his tan nose, wiping it clean, and dragged her tongue clear over his face and up around his ears.

I didn't need the shears. The umbilical cord had broken of itself when Babe swung around. The frayed end hung from the calf's belly. Babe kept washing him, in great sweeps of her tongue. On neck and flanks his tawny fur rippled like sand on a lake bottom. "I'll call him Sandy," I decided.

He rested on his side under his mother's caresses. An immense feeling overwhelmed me as I gazed around. Cobwebs hung in dusty clumps, gilded by lantern light. The barn was hushed except for an occasional stamp from the horse stalls and the sound of their eating.

The calf was dry now. Babe looked at him calmly as he raised himself on spindly legs that seemed to break apart when he tried to stand. When he did make it, she thrust out her tongue and with a lick tumbled him flat. He got right up again, and took a wobbly step. He swayed, caught his balance, then took another. His mother licked him, but this time he didn't fall. He moved to her side and put his head in under her flank and started to nurse, his short tail wagging. He stamped his baby hooves and butted his mother's bag with his mite of a nose.

Tired out, I went in the house. I knelt, and with all my heart I thanked God for Sandy. I asked forgiveness for all the sins I could remember and promised that I would try to live up to Sandy.

In the morning, long before the sky paled into dawn, I carried the steaming teakettle to the barn. The night's happening seemed like a dream now. But as I lit the lantern and walked over to the pen I found the calf there with his mother. She stood protectively while he slept on the straw. When he heard me he opened his eyes and scrambled to his feet. He braced himself, thrust out his muzzle and yawned, showing his bluish tongue and the pink of his gums.

I poured hot water over bran and stirred Babe's mash. She curved her tongue over her nose and mooed. Sandy toddled over, butted into her bag and sucked. He got so much milk that it ran out the corners of his mouth and down his chin. Mama'd told me I'd have to tie Sandy outside the stall right away and get him used to drinking from a pail before the time came to use Babe's milk for ourselves. I made a rope collar and put around his neck. He wasn't afraid of me. He grabbed onto the knee of my pants and sucked, lips clamped tight. Feet straddled, flanks going in and out, he thumped my knee hard and wagged his tail like a puppy. I smoothed down his ears and ran both hands along the sides of his neck, over his shoulders clear back to his thighs. When I touched his tail he jerked it indignantly.

I led Babe to her stall and fastened her in the stanchion. Sandy followed me. He put his head down and smelled the cement floor, then galloped across it in stiff-legged leaps. At the gutter he stumbled and sprawled headlong, but he got right up and landed next his mother, who shook her stanchion and craned her neck with anxious lows.

When I tried to lead Sandy away he stuck out his front feet and braced them hard. I had to drag him across the gutter, over the concrete and up to the wall, where I tied him short to an upright. I spread an armful of clean straw under him and stood back to watch. He blinked his eyes and stared back at me curiously. He was full of wonder about everything around him.

Mama stepped in the door. "Where is he?" she asked.

"There! Isn't he pretty?"

She walked over and put her hand out to Sandy. He grabbed her stubby fingers and sucked. Mama pushed him away and wiped her wet hand on her apron. "Yes, he's real pretty. Reminds me of a calf Papa had when I was little. I named him Brownie. Papa told me not to set my heart on him, for he'd be sold soon. And he was, too, before he was weaned. You'll have to sell this one, you know. Too bad it's not a heifer we could raise to replace old Babe."

"I won't sell him," I said. "I'll keep him for a pet. Maybe I can break him to skid logs like they did in the old days. He'll be an ox."

"You're talking foolish," said Mama. "Keep his feed pail scalded good, so he won't get scours." She went over to knead Babe's bag with her fingers. "Feels all right," she said. "Watch it doesn't harden up on you. Make sure you strip her clean every time. You start teaching him to drink. It's not an easy job, but it's easier if he's not used to sucking. He shouldn't have stayed with the cow last night."

"But he loves to suck."

"He's got to drink from a pail. Go to it now, while I get breakfast." She went back in the house.

I took the heavy pail over to where Sandy pulled against the rope. He bawled. Babe mooed. When I came close Sandy grabbed the front of my shirt and sucked. I yanked my shirt away and put my fingers in his mouth. His gums gripped hard and his rough tongue folded around my fingers. He stamped his deerlike feet and waved his tail. His face was wild as a fawn's, his eyes big and dark as a flying squirrel's. Over his shoulders his tawny coat rippled like autumn grass blown by the wind.

The pail was between us. Sandy didn't notice the milk in the pail. He was busy sucking my fingers. He butted my hand like he'd butted his mother's bag. The more he couldn't get milk the harder he butted. I lowered my hand into the milk. His nose went with it, but when it plunged into the milk he sputtered and coughed. He threw up his head and reached for my shirt. Every time I lured his nose into the milk he ended up choking. He grew frantic as he kept tasting milk but couldn't find it. Finally, I learned to stop my hand when his lips touched the milk and he began to slurp it up.

That night I watched him drink. He had all four feet braced like a giraffe drinking. His head was in the pail while his tail snapped to and fro. He didn't know he was a veal calf. His innocence broke my heart. I tried to think that Sandy was perfection; that nothing could touch him. But I knew better. When the chores were finished I took a last look at him standing in the lantern light, his shadow thrown on the rough stable wall. Then I saw down his face a raw red welt where something had raked him. Blood oozed over his nose and dripped onto the straw. On the wall a nail stuck out, and it held a tuft of his hair.

I pounded the nail in with my boot heel. I rubbed my face against his neck and said, "I'm sorry."

When I told Mama that Sandy had been hurt on his first day of life she sniffed. "He's in the school of hard knocks, like us all," she said. "Nobody gets through life without a scratch."

In early May, as the bluebirds made their nests while I plowed the fields, the man came to take Sandy away. He stepped from his slatted truck. "Where's the calf?" he asked. I went in the barn. When Sandy saw me his ears perked up and he pulled against the rope. Babe was in the pasture. I was glad she wouldn't see.

The man undid the rope. I wanted to holler, "No!" and stop him. Instead I watched him lead Sandy out into the sun, along to the truck. Sandy was eager to go. He sniffed the air and pointed his ears. My hands stayed still as if they were tied, while the man pushed him quickly up the ramp to sprawl on dirty straw. He slammed the door. Sandy scrabbled to his feet and bawled to me. The man handed me a five and a ten. "Fifteen, that's right, isn't it?" he said, climbed into his ramshackle truck and drove away.

It wasn't right, but I didn't know what to do. Like Judas, I had taken the money and betrayed the innocent.

Bracken

MAMA had two boarders that summer. One was Irene, eleven; the other was Mrs. Kessler, an old German woman. She was a gray mole who scurried short-sightedly, her eyes magnified behind thick lenses, but she saw everything.

Irene was pale and pretty, with a passion for nursing. She even had a play nursing kit and books about care of the sick. And she loved cats above everything.

One morning when I let the cow in she put her head through the stanchion and gave a "Whoosh!" of suspicion. I latched the stanchion and rushed around to the manger. There lay Gretel, my yellow cat, with three kittens. Two were gray, the other black and white. Their fur was wet and plastered down, their tails like strings and their eyes tight shut. Gretel lay on her side, half-curled around the kittens, who mewed in thin squeals.

Gretel's eyes shone golden in her furry face with the white whiskers. Her body shuddered and she groaned.

Another kitten, bloody and string-tailed, slipped from under her tail. This one was yellow like her, and covered with slime. Gretel turned and licked the kitten vigorously, her ridged pink tongue like a rough washcloth. She licked the slime and swallowed it, blood and all. She licked the others too, and washed the hay. Soon the hay was clean and the kittens' hair had begun to fluff out. They crawled to her breast, found the teats and began to suck. Gretel lay back. She purred. Her side rose and fell, as the kittens sucked and kneaded her breast with their paws.

The cow stood, legs straddled, head down, to watch and listen. After a snort or two she snatched a wisp of hay and began to eat, her eyes rolled sideways toward the cats.

When I told Irene about the kittens she was wild. "I never saw a kitten born," she wailed. "Why didn't you tell me?"

"It was over almost, when I got there." To mollify her I said, "You can have the kittens if you take them up to the loft and feed Gretel for me. The kittens'll be yours, but Gretel's still mine."

Irene sat watching the sleeping kittens as I milked Babe. Gretel walked round and round a post. She rubbed against it, purring. I tilted a teat and squeezed to send a spurt of milk toward her. It struck her full in the face. She didn't mind. She opened her mouth, held her head forward and caught the stream expertly. She smacked her lips. When she was satisfied I settled down to milk with two hands. The milk foamed up the sides of the pail. Chub and Mabe stirred, waiting for their grain. Gretel and Irene talked to the kittens. The barn even without Sandy was full of life.

I had never picked so many wild strawberries as I did that summer. In one field where rocky outcrops lay exposed to the sun, dwarf stems held berries the size of my thumb nail. Daisies and blue-eyed grass grew everywhere and bobolinks sprang from among them, bubbling their mixed-up song. Field sparrows nested there, and meadowlarks; snakes slithered through the weeds and rabbits browsed. Every day during the season I rode Chub over there, tied him under a tree and picked. Mama canned the berries as a gourmet item for the school. She made huge shortcakes too, serving half to each of us as our only food at supper. Over the shortcake we heaped whipped cream from our cow.

It was an extravagant summer, but winter was coming. I tried to get ready. I decided to cut poverty grass for hay. The tough grass with its prickly blades grew on deserted farms all up and down our road. I cut with a sickle, for it grew in spreading clumps which a scythe would not cut. With a wooden rake I brought the hay together in windrows for loading. A day's work made only a paltry jag on the wagon. After two weeks I stopped cutting poverty grass. I had found something better.

Clean bright straw for bedding was expensive, but the horses and cow had to have it. As I galloped through the pasture one day I had noticed for the first time the stand of bracken that covered an acre or more. Nothing else grew so prolifically, yet the stock did not eat it. I wondered why farmers didn't use brakes for bedding.

With a scythe I mowed great swathes. As the curved blade moved against the stems it cut them clean and dragged them into rows. Step, swing! Step, swing! My rhythm grew smooth. By night I had half the patch done. This was only a start. From deserted farms I could gather acres of brakes and have all the bedding I needed.

The brakes dried fast. At chore time I spread the fluffy gray-green fronds over the stall floors. When the horses stepped, it crackled. The more they stepped the more it released its fragrance, like pine needles warmed by the sun.

I told Mama about my find. "They've been there all the time, wasted," I said. "They're just as good as straw."

"I never heard of anyone using brakes for bedding," said Mama. "Your grandpa farmed all his life and he never did."

"He had plenty of straw," I said. "It takes a long time to cut them. But I don't mind. If I keep at it I'll have enough for all winter."

"There must be a reason why nobody uses brakes," she said. But I had learned to ignore some things Mama said.

One evening when the chores were done I watched the horses feed. Chub had finished his oats and he burrowed into his manger to pick out choice bits of hay. He stepped back, put his head down and picked up a mouthful of brakes. He chewed them with vigor and reached for more. I put an armful in his manger. He ate it ravenously. Strange, he never touched it when it was growing. I offered some to Mabe, but she turned it down. Maybe she was too old, or the stems too tough.

June passed into July. I was harvesting brakes from far up the road. Chub ate about half hay and half brakes now. One morning when I backed him out of his stall he stumbled. At the threshold he floundered across and almost fell.

I led him up to Mabe, fastened the crosslines and

stepped back. "Giddup!" I said. Chub jumped ahead. As they turned the corner of the barn he lurched sidewise and leaned drunkenly against Mabe. Were his feet hurt? I lifted his feet one by one, but they seemed all right.

We trotted off to a plowing job three miles away. In rough footing, Chub stumbled and at corners he swayed against the wagon pole. Still he kept on, and when I'd hitched them to the plow he pulled as always. He wavered going around the ends of furrows, but at noon he ate his oats and drank a pail of water.

Through the long afternoon we kept working. At dusk the piece was finished. I loaded the plow and hitched up to go home. Chub acted tired, but he ate a good supper. As I milked I could hear him chew. "They're all right if they can eat," Grandpa used to say.

At supper I told Mama how Chub had acted. "It'll pass," she said. "Don't worry, he's young and healthy. Maybe something he ate."

Next morning I hurried to the stable. He looked all right, but when I curried him he shifted his feet as though I'd pushed him. Later as comb and brush pressed his shoulder he fell against the partition. With an effort he recovered, then tottered the other way. His weight crushed me against the wall. He spread his legs to steady himself. He shook his head. When I led him out his legs buckled and he almost fell. As we harrowed the field he lurched this way and that like a man in deep sand. We finished the job before noon. On the way home Chub swayed around the curves. I had seven dollars, our pay for the job. It would take three dollars to pay for a vet, plus medicine he might prescribe. If I spent the money there'd be nothing left for feed.

I had to tell Mama. "Chub's worse. Should we have the doctor?"

"Nonsense. He isn't down yet. We can't pay a doctor for every little thing."

"But he's not eating." Chub hadn't touched his oats that noon. He stood listless now, his legs trembling, head down. His eyes were sunken and dull.

"It's a bad sign, his not eating," she said. "But he may not be really sick. Suppose he ate something that disagreed with him. He'll work it off."

Something he ate? I remembered what Chub had eaten that Mabe had not. Brakes! I rushed to the barn. Chub was still on his feet and his ears pricked halfway as I walked in beside him. He made an effort to move over, and leaned against the partition as if he were tired. I threw my arms around his neck and hugged him, then I clawed out every bit of bracken from his manger and stall.

"I'm sorry." I held his head with both hands, shut my eyes and prayed, "Please, God, make him well. If I've done wrong don't take it out on Chub."

That afternoon I hitched him to the cultivator and made him work. He no longer fought the lines or snorted, or arched his neck. Instead he plodded like an old horse, his tail clamped to his body. "Please, God, please." For three hours I kept him going. There were only six rows left when he stumbled and fell on his side, flattening a row of beans. I've killed him! I thought. I undid the traces and loosened his collar. His tongue lolled in the dirt, his tail lay limp. He breathed hard, his eyes closed.

The sun was hot. Water! I ran to the creek and snatched off my shirt. I laid the dripping cloth over his forehead and down around his throat. I wanted to ride Mabe for the doctor, but I couldn't leave Chub to lie in the dirt. I bent over and gave our old signal for speed. "S-s-s-s!"

He raised his head, opened his eyes. A shudder ran through him. With a bound he got to his feet. He shook himself, then walked unsteadily to the stable, where I rubbed him down and left him standing.

After supper when I went out to milk I heard a whinny. Chub had finished his oats and was coaxing for more. "That's enough," I scolded. "Now eat your hay."

Hate and Sympathy

It was Sunday morning. I planned to pull stumps and make a bed for strawberries. But first came worship. Mama read from Job 28 about the path that no fowl knoweth, the lion's whelps and the vulture's eye. When she came to the ending, "Behold, the fear of the Lord, that is wisdom; and to depart from evil is understanding," my mind was full of pictures of vultures soaring and lions creeping behind rocks. She said, "Let us pray." We knelt on the linoleum, Mrs. Kessler first on her knees. In a loud mumble she spoke to God in German while my mind rambled over the desert, then back to the stumps and the strawberries. Outside a robin sang. Mrs. Kessler's voice droned on. My legs twitched. I opened my eyes and saw Irene by the chair next to me, hands clasped like a saint.

When the guttural monologue ceased, Mama began. After her came my turn, then Irene's. The moment Irene said Amen I jumped up and hustled to the barn to hitch up the team. While I worked a brown thrasher sang in a big maple by the stone wall and chipmunks scampered among the stones. Whenever we got close to the maple the thrasher left his perch and dropped like a dried leaf into the brush along the wall. He skulked and called, "Chack! Chack!" and I knew he had a nest nearby. Bluebirds came to investigate what we were doing. As soon as a stump was pulled they alighted in the hole to pick up insects.

Mama had driven over to see Uncle Lewis. At noon I strode into the house expecting dinner. Irene was sprawled on the living room floor cutting paper dolls. Mrs. Kessler in her cubbyhole off the kitchen sang a German hymn. The table wasn't set and on the stove was nothing but the teakettle.

"Why didn't you get dinner?" I yelled at Irene.

"It's not my job," she said as her scissors shaped a paper dress.

"Well, I can't do two jobs at once. I've been out pulling stumps all morning. Mama said you're to help with meals."

"She's not *my* mother," said Irene. She folded flaps over the doll's shoulders. "Besides, my father pays board."

"You get off the floor and get busy," I said.

"I don't have to mind you." She rose and idled toward the kitchen. "Is Mrs. Kessler eating with us?" she asked.

"Let her eat when she gets ready," I said. Before we sat down, however, Mrs. Kessler's door flew open and she charged in, gray hair flying. She scampered to her chair, gave the table a myopic stare and muttered, "Yah! Yah! Just like my own children. No respect. If you want respect, go find it in the dictionary." She got a plate for herself and dished a share of the food we'd prepared.

With a wink at Irene I said to Mrs. Kessler, "We thought you were asleep."

"Yah, sleep," she mimicked. "Old woman sleep. No see what goes on. I see how you treat your mother."

"I treat her as well as she treats me," I said.

"Ach! God will pay you. Your mother is too good to you."

"At least she has sympathy, which is more than you've got."

"T-r-r-r-r-t!" she said harshly. "Sympathy! You find that in the dictionary."

Irene kept right on eating without a word. I gulped my food and left them at the table—the too-old and the too-young.

When I came in from chores that evening Mama took me aside. "Mrs. Kessler says you were rude to her today."

"She was mad because we didn't set a place for her," I said.

"You talked back to her, she says."

"Well, she was rude first. Said we had no respect."

"Now, look here," Mama said. "Mrs. Kessler's a boarder. I need her money. Also she's our guest. She's an old lady and you must treat her with respect."

"But Mama, she's stupid and she talks in German when she knows I can't understand. She's always telling me I'm like her own kids. She hates them, and she hates me too. Well, I hate her!"

"Don't talk like that. You mustn't hate."

"I do, though. I can't help it."

"Pray to God to help you," she said. "Meanwhile, don't let me hear again of your being snippy to Mrs. Kessler. She's a poor old woman without any family to go to and she needs our sympathy."

"Sympathy! She says you can find that in the dictionary."

"It's something you have to develop," said Mama. "What if you were old like her, without a home?"

"She'd have a home if her children liked her," I said. "It's all her fault."

"You've got a lot to learn," said Mama. "Don't be disrespectful again or I'll have to punish you." When Mama kissed me goodnight I turned my head away. Before I blew out my light I roamed the room kicking at the rug like Satan seeking whom he may devour. My sympathy was with Satan. Everyone picked on him. God had the power to kill me, though, so I had to make peace with Him. I tried to read, but I couldn't. I slammed the book and crept down the stairs. Under the stars I fled to the barn where the horses were. I leaned against Chub's neck in the warm darkness. After a while I went back to my room and knelt beside the bed. "Don't let me be mean to Mrs. Kessler anymore," I begged. Don't let her be mean to me was what I meant, but God wouldn't like that.

The next day I escaped again to my different world: the friendly bluebirds, the willing horses, the blessed stones, earth and stumps. I saw Irene headed for the barn. She was going to play with the kittens, which she'd taken from the cow's manger and put up in the loft. They had begun to crawl around in the hay.

Before I'd cleared the first stump Irene ran toward me. "Something's the matter!" she gasped. "The kittens can't see. They were all right last night. Now—"

"Well, they're your cats, you take care of them. You're the nurse," I said crossly.

"But I don't know what to do."

I threw down my ax. We climbed the ladder to the hayloft, where the kittens lay in a mewing heap, Gretel stretched beside them. She kneaded the hay and purred as I knelt to examine her kittens. I held one up, finger under his chin. His blue eyes were sealed shut. All the kittens were afflicted. Irene held the black and white one close to her face, which was wet with tears.

"What can't be cured must be endured," I quoted glibly. A hard lump had moved to my throat. "Maybe they can be cured, though." Gretel's purr rumbled softly. The kittens' mews were thin and weak. Like a madonna, Irene held the blind kitten, her blonde hair a halo about her face.

"I'll ask Mama," I said. I left Irene to comfort the kittens and went in the house. Mama continued to scrub the floor as I told her about the kittens. "Wash them with boric acid," she said. "That's soothing and it heals. They'll be all right." She rose, rinsed her hands and went to the cupboard stocked with bandages, peroxide and castor oil. "Pshaw! There's none here. I'll get some when I go to town."

"When?"

"Maybe tomorrow," she said. She closed the cupboard and got back on her knees.

"That'll be too late!"

"It's the best I can do."

At the kitchen table Mrs. Kessler was picking over beans. She peered closely with her half-blind eyes. "Fuss, fuss over animals," she muttered. "No respect for people." She didn't see the look I gave her.

"I'll go," I said. "I'll go on Chub."

Two hours later I brought the medicine home. Mama had the water hot. She told me to put a teaspoonful of powder in a glass of boiled water. When it had dissolved and the liquid had cooled I took a roll of cotton and the bowl of solution to the mow. There sat Irene, all four kittens asleep on her lap while she crooned to them. I took up the gray kitten, dipped cotton in the lukewarm boric acid and began to sponge off his face. I dripped the medicine over his tight-shut lids. With needle claws he tried to push me away. Irene dabbed at the black and white one's face. A half hour later all eight eyes were bathed. Gretel licked each face, washing the medicine off.

"I hope enough got inside," I said. "Make the solution fresh every day. And bathe their eyes three times a day. Don't you dare miss once. You want them to get well, don't you?"

Irene wanted to sleep near the kittens. I asked Mama if we could both sleep in the barn. "All right," she said. "But don't let me call you twice in the morning."

That night Irene and I took pillows and blankets and slept above the stable, under the loft where the kittens were. Beyond us gapped the bay, where our buggy and sleigh were crowded against tangled wrecks of old farm machinery. From one corner we could look the other way through cracks to see the winking stars. We lay in prickly hay and giggled and talked, until our voices were cut short by a rumble of thunder so strong it shook the beams. A flash lit up the inside of the barn. The stars were gone. Rain thudded on the roof. Thunder came again, and lightning blazed like fireworks. It snapped and fizzed. Rain sluiced down. It drummed above our heads and ran in sheets from the eaves.

A brilliant flash showed Mabe and Chub standing with heads bowed, tails tucked in, under a maple next to the road. I didn't know where Babe was. She was out in it too.

I remembered that I hadn't said my prayers. I had been mean to Mrs. Kessler and bullied Irene. If God got even, I'd deserve it. Buff had been lying in the hay near us. At the first crack of thunder he yelped and crawled beside me. Nose pressed into my thigh, he shivered and whined and tried to make himself small. "Don't be scared," I said. I reached out a hand that trembled and patted his head.

"Lightning victims do recover," said Irene. "If a person's struck, use artificial respiration to restore breathing and keep victim warm." She talked as though she were reading from a book.

"If lightning hits you, you drop dead," I said. "Remember Mr. Cleaver driving his team to the barn? He lay dead in the field while his horses rammed the barn door, trying to get in. And how about the Turner boys camped under the big hickory? Killed all four. I wish Mabe and Chub would get out from under that tree."

In the morning the sky was clear. Rain drops sparkled on the leaves, the creek flowed fast and deep. Chub and Mabe grazed calmly up the slope.

That night the stars were out when we entered the barn. Irene threw a pillow that hit me right in the face. I raised mine over one shoulder and pitched it straight for her. She ducked and the pillow whizzed past, snagged a nail and white feathers exploded. We shrieked with laughter. I doubled over and held onto aching sides while the feathers floated zigzag, like lazy snow, onto our heads.

"Girls!" a shout came. "Stop that noise! I want to get some sleep."

"All right, Mama," I hollered. Irene covered her mouth with her hands to keep from laughing. I smothered mine with a blanket. We moved close together and started to talk once more. It was time to discuss our great adventure.

"Will your mother let us do it?" Irene whispered.

I thought of Mama's iron face; her will, the will of God. "She's got to," I said.

The Great Adventure

AT BREAKFAST I announced, "Irene and I want to ride up to Aunt Emma's."

"That's impossible," said Mama. "It's a hundred and fifty miles. It'd take you a week."

"That's all right. We'll stay overnight outdoors."

"What about feed for the horses?"

"We'll carry some with us. We'll buy more on the way. Besides, they'll eat grass along the way."

"What about Irene? What'll you do if she gets sick?"

"She never gets sick."

"I'll think about it," said Mama. She got up from the table, found her handbag and lifted a pail of wallpaper paste. "You girls better show me you're responsible before I let you go off alone," she said. "Do the dishes, Irene."

"Yes, ma'am," said Irene. She jumped up to start the dishes.

At supper I asked, "Mama, we can go, can't we?"

"I guess you can," she said. "But what about the crops?"

"We won't go till August when they're laid by. And we'll be back in time for harvest."

"How're you going to ride?" said Mama. "You've got no saddles."

"Kitty French has a Western she said she'd lend me and Mr. Boyes has an old army saddle. He wanted to sell it, but maybe he'll lend it."

August came. The crops were cultivated for the last time. It was the night before we were to start. Irene and I made peanut butter sandwiches in the kitchen. "We'll put these in the horses' grain bags and tie them behind the saddles," I said.

"How about water?"

"I've got a canteen Laurance gave me. We can both drink from it."

"Are we going to take Buff?" Irene asked.

"Sure. We'll be real westerners with our dog trotting along."

"Your mother said she'd feed Gretel and the kittens, and milk the cow. At least she won't have to take care of Buff and the horses. Or us. Mrs. Kessler won't have many dishes to do. Or anyone to scold."

"Grumpy old witch," I said. "She'll have to talk to herself."

As the sun rose over the woods the following morning, Irene and I gave our cinches a last pull. Buff circled the horses and jumped to lick their noses. He had a big grin on his face. At the door stood Mama. She had already kissed us goodbye. "Should you go, girls?" she asked, her arms hugged over her breast. "You'll swelter, and it's a long way."

"Don't worry, Mama." I jumped into the saddle lest she still say no.

"I shouldn't let you go." She wrung her hands. From behind her peered the wizened face of Mrs. Kessler.

"Ach! Some people don't know. Young girls, away from home—"

"Goodbye, Mama," I said. "See you in September." We waved. The horses trotted off. Buff frisked ahead.

A half mile up the road I pulled Chub in where the creek crossed under. Irene and Mabe were far behind. The sun's rays sparkled on a sleeping caterpillar, making each tuft of him glisten. As Mabe lumbered up I snapped, "Come on, we haven't got all day." My voice sounded like Mama's. "We've got to make fifty miles before night."

"Well, I can't help it if Mabe's slow," said Irene.

We trotted on. We passed through Camden, where Mama did her weekly shopping, then ahead into unexplored territory. The sun dried the dew. The birds stopped singing. Buff scared up sparrows and towhees where they rested in the brush. Farmers cut rowen in the hayfields and reaped grain already ripe. Meadowlarks called from the fenceposts. We came into Williamstown.

"Whew! It's hot," Irene said, standing up in her stirrups. "I'm hungry."

"No sandwiches till noon," I said. A few miles past Williamstown a brook ran through a meadow. The horses turned toward it, and Buff waded in lapping. Then he lay right down and with his tongue took swipes at the water while his tail sloshed back and forth. Stiffly, Irene and I knelt and splashed cool water over our heads.

"My seat's sore and my legs are lame," said Irene.

"We've just started. You can't get lame now," I said. "Toughen up."

We fed the horses in our hats and sat near them to eat. Buff devoured pieces of peanut-butter sandwich, then lay in the shade to sleep. The horses grazed as we held their ropes.

After an hour I said, "Saddle up." We threw on the damp blankets and lifted the heavy saddles. "I'm too weak to get back on," said Irene as she leaned against Mabe.

"Fiddlesticks. Hop to it, or I'll leave you behind."

By mid-afternoon the horses were more tired than I'd ever seen them. I had to urge Chub on, and his trot soon petered out to a walk. Mabe plodded along as though her feet were hobbled. A stand of giant sugar maples loomed ahead. "We'll go in there for the night," I said, and we pulled off the road.

"I'm thirsty," said Irene as she crawled off her horse.

"Me too," I said. "And I never knew what saddle-weary meant before."

I dragged Chub's saddle off and let it thud to the ground, took off his bridle and led him by the halter to a stream that gurgled over stones. While Chub drank I squatted to cup water in both hands, then threw myself on the gravel and buried my mouth. Downstream Buff lay up to his elbows and lapped.

Irene came with Mabe. "Don't let her have too much," I warned.

"I know. You don't have to tell me."

"Don't be snippy."

The horses rolled, then grazed through deep grass while we held their ropes and ate sandwiches. Heat simmered even after the sun was gone. A flock of crows cawed over. Cicadas shrilled from the maple branches. Up ahead a farmer called his cows.

"We'll have to buy bread tomorrow," I said as I threw a crust to Buff.

"Jelly too," said Irene.

With saddles for pillows we lay on dry leaves and pulled up the sweaty blankets. "This blanket's itchy," said Irene.

"Be quiet." I curled tight and tried to sleep. Mosquitoes came in swarms. Roots and stones gouged me until sleep put an end to my misery.

The sun came up bright. Birds sang. Cicadas tuned up again. We gulped handfuls of chokecherries for breakfast and started on. We both stood in the stirrups, so the saddles would not hit legs and seat in the same spots as before. Ten miles to the next town! It was nearly noon before we got there. We bought two loaves of bread and a jar of jelly.

Buff loped on the shady side of the horses. He no longer circled through the brush, but veered hopefully into every ditch and dry streambed. At last we saw a farmhouse ahead. It was white with green shutters and was surrounded by leafy trees and shady lawn. We rode up to the barn. A big bushy-haired man, face burned red by the sun, came to the barn door. With narrow eyes he watched us come near.

"Hello," I said. "We're thirsty. Could you please give us water?"

"Water!" he said. "Wish I had water myself. Thirty cows and every drop has to come five miles from the river. Can't haul it fast enough."

"No water?" said Irene.

"Girls, you don't know what you're asking. There's a drought on here. Water's like gold." On husky legs he stood by the great barn beside the comfortable house. His eyes were hard. "Keep on, girls," he said. "You'll find water farther on."

"Old skinflint," said Irene as we got back to the road. "I'd like to see him crawl across the desert with an empty canteen."

We came to one streambed after another—all dry. "He said five miles to the river," I said. "We should be almost there."

A crooked row of willows showed ahead. The horses pricked their ears. We came over a rise and saw a broad bed of gravel winding under willows. In the middle flowed a thread of water. My mouth tried to swallow. I wanted to shout, but when we came nearer we saw that there was no gap in the high fence that separated river and road. The fence extended right to the bridge, high above water.

"That mean man knew it," cried Irene. "He knew the river was fenced."

Chub whickered coaxingly. Buff tried to dig under the close-meshed wire.

"There's only one thing to do," I said. "We're almost to Mannsville, where Mama has friends. We can go there. It's three miles out of our way, but they'll have water."

The horses' feet fell like dropped stones on the dirt

road. Buff limped. We came over a hill and saw the house, set back from the road among clusters of trees. A herd of Holsteins moved single-file toward the barn.

When we rode in Mrs. Alber came to the door. "What on earth!" she said. "Come on in. The girls'll be happy to see you. They remember last time you were here with your mother." Two little girls ran up. "These are our daughters, Barbara and Ellen. Tie your horses under the trees. My husband'll take them to the barn when he comes in. What on earth are you two doing here on horseback? You've had a long ride."

As we sank into chairs in the kitchen Irene said, "Could I have a drink?"

"Of course. Barbara, run get glasses." She pumped water into the sink, filled two glasses and the girls brought them to us. "Another glass? My, you were thirsty." Mrs. Alber pumped again. "Didn't you find water along the way?"

"All the streams are dry," I said. "We asked one man but he said there's a drought and he didn't have any."

"Oh, the drought. Lucky our well's not dry yet."

"Our horses are thirsty," I said. "We've got a dog too."

"That's right. Barbara, show them the watering trough."

From an iron pipe water trickled into a full trough. Chub thrust his nose into the cool water, making waves wash over the sides. Mabe joined him and drew water in long wheezing gulps.

We tied the horses and sat on the lawn with the little girls. I laid my aching back on the grass, hands under my head, and looked up at the undersides of leaves. A man's voice waked me. Mr. Alber showed us stalls for the horses and threw down hay to fill the mangers. He poured two quarts of oats in each feed box.

After supper Mrs. Alber said, "You can't go on tomorrow. Stay here and rest a few days."

"We've come on the trip to rough it," I said, and I felt guilty as she showed us upstairs to an airy corner room. A cool breeze fanned our foreheads as we went to sleep.

In the morning I shook Irene. "Get up! We've got to get going."

She started up, then sank back. "My back! I can't move."

"Yes, you can. Shake a leg and let's go. We haven't got all day."

She gave me a look.

A rooster crowed. Mr. Alber drove his team to the hayfield and the hens spread out from the barnyard. The cows were on their way to pasture as we went down to breakfast.

"It's going to be a scorcher," said Mrs. Alber as she set a plate of pancakes between us. "Why don't you stay over? Maybe it'll be cooler tomorrow."

"We can't stay," I said firmly. "We've got only a few days and we're already late." After breakfast we saddled up. Mrs. Alber had made stacks of sandwiches and her husband had filled our bags with oats. Our canteen was full.

By noon my body was stiff again. The horses let their heads hang. Heat waves shimmered over the road. As the horses drifted slowly along I had time to see fields laid out on side hills, with patches of corn tall and green against the sky. Pictures everywhere. The sun burned hotter than at noon. Our canteen was empty. All that mattered was finding a drink.

Chub and Mabe moved like sleepwalkers. Buff panted as he slouched along. Something caught my eye—a sign tacked to a tree. As we rode closer I read the hand-lettered words: BUTTERMILK FOR SALE

We rode up the driveway and stopped under an elm by the back door. A woman came out on the stoop. She wiped her hands on her apron and smoothed gray hair over her ears. She looked like Grandma—short and plump with a kind wrinkled face.

I slid out of the saddle. "Could we buy two glasses of buttermilk?"

"Of course. Get down," she said to Irene. "I'll be right out." She went in the house. Irene got off and threw herself under the elm. The horses grazed and Buff panted in the shade.

The woman stepped out, a tray in her hands. She set it on the grass and handed us each a tall jelly glass. From a china pitcher beaded with moisture she poured buttermilk until the glasses were full. "Drink," she said. My lips felt creamy foam while the cold liquid flooded my throat and flecks of butter dotted my tongue. "Dig in," the woman said. She pointed to thick molasses cookies on the tray. "And drink all you want. Rest yourselves. I'll get water for your dog and horses." From a well behind the house she brought water in buckets and a granite basin for Buff.

"Now tell me why you're here and where you're going."

When I told her she said, "It's getting late. You'd be welcome to stay overnight."

"Let's," Irene spoke up.

"We have to keep going," I said. "We can get quite a ways before dark." I pulled change from my pocket. "How much do we owe you, ma'am?"

"Not a cent," she said. She pushed the money away. "You're welcome to all you can eat and drink." As I pressed it on her she backed off. "No, no. You may need it along the way." She stuffed our pockets with cookies.

By sundown we'd gone through Evans Mills and we looked for a place to sleep. It felt like rain.

"I don't want to be out in the rain," said Irene.

"I wish you hadn't come," I said.

"I wish so, too. You're a slave driver. We could have stayed at that woman's place."

"Go back then. I'm going on." I saw a squat gray building ahead. "There's a public roads shed," I said. "We'll go in there for the night." We tied the horses to the fence out back. I tried the door. It wasn't locked. We lugged our saddles in, past tractors, graders and rollers, and dumped them in a corner and went back out to let the horses graze. Buff scratched the soil under a clump of goldenrod and lay down, his red tongue hanging out. While Irene held the horses I carried our wet blankets high up a hill under a line of locusts that overlooked the road.

"I want a drink," said Irene.

"Shut up!" I snapped. "You know there's no water." I jerked Chub's rope from her hand and led him to the fence. "Tie Mabe up," I commanded. "Give her oats."

Irene obeyed. She leaned against Mabe's shoulder, her hands to her head. I knew she was crying. "Come on," I said. "Let's get some sleep."

The wet blanket scratched my face. A swarm of

mosquitoes whined. Buff crawled close to me, scared of the heat lightning that played along the horizon. Finally I went to sleep. I was awakened by violent thunder and rain pelting down. We rushed headlong down the hill. In the shed we huddled next to a giant grader blade while the horses stood outside in the rain. The long night passed.

There was no food for breakfast and no place to buy any. Irene sulked as we fed the horses and saddled up. Water lay everywhere in pools, but the sun boiled down. We got ready to go.

"Sit straight," I said to Irene as she slumped in the saddle. "You'll get round-shouldered."

She gave me a look of pure hatred and flounced her shoulders. "See if I care."

"Don't talk back to me," I said.

"You only think of yourself," she flung out. "You don't pity anyone else."

"If you want pity, find it in the dictionary," I said. The words sounded familiar. My voice was Mrs. Kessler's and the words were hers. I looked into Irene's small defiant face. Overwhelmed, I saw myself.

Buff lay under the goldenrod, all four feet stretched out. I saw blood on his pads. "Look at Buff," I said. We forgot our anger and got down to examine his feet. I fingered his worn pads. He thumped his tail.

"What'll we do?" asked Irene.

"I don't know. He'll have to keep going somehow." Buff limped along on three legs. When we bought peanut butter and bread at a crossroads store we offered him some, but he nosed it away. In late afternoon he lay down in a puddle and refused to move. "Buff!" I called.

His ears cocked half way, he started to stand, then lay back and lowered his ears. He whimpered. "Buff, you come here!" I said sternly. He dragged himself up, his tail tight between his legs.

We'd come to the higher country around Richville and DeKalb, and beside us flowed the Oswegatchie River while in the hilly fields rose boulders and outcroppings of rocks. The boulders gave me an idea. "We'll boost Buff up on Mabe, and take turns riding Chub." I led Mabe to a tall rock. Irene helped hoist Buff up and from there ease him onto Mabe's saddle. He teetered and his claws slipped on the leather. He slid to the ground. We tried again. "Hang on," I said, but he slithered off like a sack of meal. Thunderheads stacked themselves over the timbered hillsides. The sun got low and lightning played among the clouds. "We'd better get in somewhere," said Irene.

We turned into a farmyard. From the weathered barn a man walked toward us, a brimming pail of milk in each hand. His form was stocky in faded overalls. Over his forehead fell a shock of gray hair. He saw us and said, "Hello!"

"Could we sleep in your barn?" I asked.

"No. You can't sleep in my barn, but you can sleep in my house. Hold on a minute while I strain this milk." He went into the springhouse and was soon back. "Follow me," he said, and led us to the barn. "There's two empty stalls," he said. "Put your horses there."

"We've got our own oats and blankets. But we need something for our dog. His feet are sore."

"Don't worry. Mother'll take care of him. Now, you keep your oats for later. Get some from the bin. I'll throw down hay. You girls go in the house and get washed up while I finish these cows."

Water in a basin and clean fluffy towels. The smell of potatoes frying and the table set. Fresh bread and butter and applesauce and steaming sweet corn. The farmer came in and we sat down to supper. "Your dog's all right," he said. "I gave him food and water. He's under the butternut tree where it's shady."

After supper we went out to Buff. He hadn't eaten a bit. When we put the food near him he turned away. "He don't look sick," the man said. "Maybe he'll eat in the morning. He's all tuckered out."

I insisted we sleep in the barn. The farmer showed us the ladder to the hayloft where a window opened to the west. He showed us how to shut the window if rain should come in. Buff lay below with the horses. He had soft hay under him and Vaseline on his feet. The woman had washed his pads and smoothed grease on thick with her fingers. Side by side Irene and I knelt in the hay by the window. The night had grown cool. Flashes of lightning revealed a bay horse standing near a fence back of the barn. Over our heads a bat flittered out.

"I'm scared about Buff," I said. "Wonder why he won't eat." A whine came from below. He'd heard his name.

We didn't hear the rain that night. We woke at daybreak to find the countryside drenched and limbs of the butternut strewn on the ground. Buff moved painfully on greasy feet. He drank a few laps of milk, but he wouldn't eat. Over corn flakes and milk with huckleberries, we talked about what we should do. The folks offered to keep him until we came back that way. "But then he'd have to travel all the way home," I said. "If we could get him the rest of the way he could stay until my mother came up by car."

Under the butternut tree the horses were saddled and ready. I gazed down at Buff. He looked beat. "We'll have to leave him," I said. Our bags were full of oats and sandwiches; our canteen was full. With Buff off my mind I felt free. Our fresh horses trotted out the drive.

"Look back," said Irene. There stood Buff, balanced on three legs. He whined and came toward us, ears half-mast.

"Stay there!" I commanded. His ears fell, and he dropped to his haunches. As we started on he got up and sidled after us, his sorest paw wincing each time it touched the ground.

"Wait," called the farmer's wife. "He'll only mourn if you leave him." She stood pinching her apron. "Come back. I've got an idea."

We turned back. She smiled. "How about boots?" She cut pieces of old works pants and we helped sew dog boots with soles four layers thick. She wiped off Buff's feet and covered his pads with fresh Vaseline, and tied the boots on with strips of cloth. "That'll fix him," she said.

As we started out once more, Buff picked his feet high, then stopped to undo the boots with his teeth. We'd hardly gotten out of sight of the house when he had one off. I tied it back on tighter. Irene and I took turns watching him, and getting down to tie his boots when they got loose. By noon, though, one boot was gone and the rest in shreds. He used the noon hour to work them off and was on his bare pads again.

The afternoon was a scorcher. We lingered at puddles

so Buff could cool his feet. But the moment the sun left the hills a chill came into the air. At bedtime we tied the horses to a pasture fence and slept in the open field. With a groan Buff stretched beside us and snorted and snuffed as he dreamed. A heavy dew fell and a bitter breeze sprang up. The wet blankets didn't cover us. Irene sat up. "I'm freezing," she said. "This is worse than the heat."

"Let's put Buff in the middle," I said. We huddled against him, but still couldn't get warm. Long before daylight we saddled up and moved on, soaked to the skin. Behind a country church we found a hitching shed and crept into a corner out of the wind. In the morning when the first rooster crowed we started on.

That night we spent in a grove of spruce whose boughs kept out the wind. The next morning we started on the last lap. At sundown we trailed into Aunt Emma's yard. Uncle Fred came out, fussing, and took the horses to the barn. Aunt Emma and Aunt Clara welcomed us in. I got Buff to the back porch and put milk in front of him. He stretched out stiff on the rough floor, his tongue hanging out like a red rag. The lamp flickered on his tongue. I knelt to get a good look, and saw that it was swollen to twice its normal size and was a deep blazing red.

I called Aunt Emma. "I've found out what's the matter with Buff," I told her. "His tongue's sunburned."

"Sunburned!" said Aunt Emma. "I never heard of such a thing." She peered down. "Well, I declare, no wonder he wouldn't eat. Let him rest now."

He slept on the porch all night. Under a tree he slept all the next day. At supper he ate a bowl of bread and milk. In three days his pads were healed, his tongue well. When Irene and I left a week later he grinned and let us go.

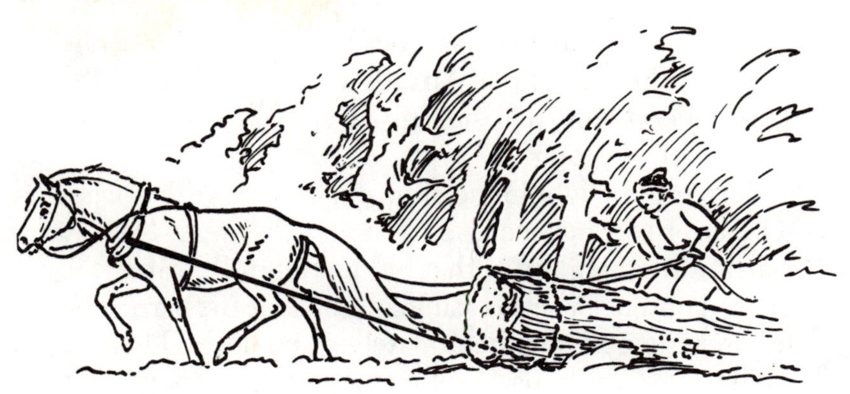

The Jigsaw

In September Mrs. Kessler and Irene both left. Laurance went back to school. I got a job skidding logs for Jake Simpson, who lived five miles away. Mama had been with me when I got the job. She'd driven up in the Willys and talked with Mr. Simpson. He'd agreed on fifty cents an hour, the going rate for a skid horse and driver.

"Almost five dollars a day! That's a fortune," I said to Mama on the way home.

"Not exactly. Nine hours' work means a lot of grain. And that long drive will wear out his shoes. I don't like you working for that man. He swears a blue streak."

"It doesn't matter. I won't learn to swear."

"That wife of his is a poor stick. I saw dirt swept into a corner. You won't be eating there, though. You'll take your own food."

"Oh Mama. You're so afraid of germs!"

"Cleanliness is next to godliness," she said. "It's a godless household you're going into."

It was early December. November snow had melted and the buggy bounced over rocks and frozen clods. The pre-dawn air was chilly. Already the sky had faded the stars. Woods on each side made a moving pattern as Chub trotted along.

There was a light in the Simpson barn as we drove up. The door was pushed open and a twelve-year-old boy came out, struggling with a full pail of milk. "Shut the door, dammit!" a bellow came from inside the barn. The boy set the milk down and latched the door. Then he went toward the house, leaning to one side to balance his load. I hitched Chub to a pear tree and opened the barn door. "What now!" Mr. Simpson's voice boomed. "You'll be late for—Oh, it's you," he said in a changed voice. "I thought it was the boy." He glanced at a battered clock on a dusty shelf. "You're on time, at least." His jaws worked on a cud of tobacco under his stubbly beard. Over pale puffy cheeks his blue eyes peered as though studying a new breed of stock. "Never had a woman work for me," he said. "Not in the woods. Think you can do it?"

"Sure. I've skidded plenty of logs. I don't mind hard work."

Outdoors he said, "That him?" when he saw Chub. "You won't move *my* logs with that little squirt."

"He can do it."

"Humph. We'll see. Unhitch, now, while I turn out my cows."

Chub had on his work harness and all I had to do was unhitch him from the buggy and attach the singletree and chain. Chub tossed his head and bunched his feet. "Whoa," I said. "You'll get plenty of work in a minute."

Mr. Simpson emerged from the barn with a one-man crosscut saw in one hand, a two-bitted ax in the other. He looked at Chub. "He'll simmer down fast," he said. "Follow me."

Through the pasture up through an old clearing he led the way into a grove of ancient pines. From the wind-swept pasture we entered a shadowy place where our footsteps were muffled. Chub's feet padded along the trail. The chain snaked behind him. At last we came to the place where Mr. Simpson had been felling. Before me stretched an acre or more of tangled trees sliced as by a giant cleaver. "Beauties, ain't they?" said Mr. Simpson. "The guy loads from the back road. Go to that far side to start. You'll have to make your own skid-trails. Enough there to keep you busy? I'll start cutting."

I found the path out to the road and backed Chub to the nearest log. The butt was almost a yard through and sound as a dollar. I slipped on the chain. "Come on, Chub!" One bound and the chain tightened, snapped him back. I angled him off and tried again. He shook his head, dug in, shortening his steps. The chain, hooked low, lifted the butt and inch by inch the log moved. It swung from its resting place and headed into the trail.

At noon I ate my dinner with Chub. Mr. Simpson hadn't asked me in. I didn't care. I'd rather eat outdoors. I held a frozen bean sandwich in my mittened hand and when I got too cold I went into the barn. There were three stanchions for cows and a stall for a heifer. A week's manure lay in the gutter. At 12:30 Mr. Simpson came out. Back in the woods time flew. At 4:30, when it was dark, I'd put in nine hours. Four-fifty earned already. Chub would have to eat extra and he'd wear out more shoes, but he was earning his keep and I'd have enough to try saving once more for school.

As I hitched up, Mr. Simpson came to the buggy. "Beats all, a woman working in the woods," he said. "But you did all right. Be here at seven sharp." He went into the barn. Chub headed for home at a dead run.

I told Mama about my day. "Did that man use swear words with you?" she asked.

"He swore a few times, but not at me."

"Did you go in the house? Did you eat with them?"

"No, Mama. He didn't ask me in."

"That's good," she said with relief. "Those folks are trash. I wish you didn't have to work there, but it's a little money coming in." Mama had something else in mind. "Did that man try any—foolishness with you?"

"Of course not. You know I'd never stand for that."

The following morning at four when I went out to feed the horses I felt snow in the air. During the day big flakes floated down. Snow would make the work harder in some ways, but I liked driving the ski-sled better than the buggy. During the night the wind rose and thick snow fell. I drove to work in a whitened world. Chub pounced like a kitten through the deep drifts, making the light sleigh jerk and sway. Gradually snow-light turned to daylight. Vague shapes of trees appeared. We arrived at the pear tree as Mr. Simpson opened the barn door and came through with two pails of milk. "Hello," he said. "Didn't think you'd make it. You go on, I'll be there."

Chub broke trail and I followed, snow to the tops of my boots. In the dim interior of the big timber, snow drifted in silence below the roaring of the wind high above.

On the other side the ugly slashing was mounded deep while over it whirled the snow. I found a log by its tomblike shape, dug away snow at the butt and fastened the chain. Mr. Simpson came and began to fell. I could hear the sound of the crosscut and an occasional, "Damn it to hell!" when a falling tree lodged. I was glad Mama couldn't hear him.

I had asked Mama once if she had a temper. She was often exasperated but she never lost her temper or swore. "Temper? We've got to control it. And to swear is a sin. Remember, God will not hold him guiltless that taketh His name in vain."

"But don't you get mad?" I had to know if Mama was different from me.

"Yes, things make me mad," she admitted. Her chin was propped with her hand as she gazed at the floor. She tossed her head and flung out her hands. "I feel sometimes I'd like to tear everything to pieces and swear a blue streak!" Abruptly she composed her face and admonished, "We all sin and come short of the glory of God. We have to ask forgiveness and keep trying."

"But, Mama, why's it all right to say 'mad as a hornet,' and a sin to say 'mad as—you know—'? Isn't it being angry that counts?"

"Anger itself is wrong, but sometimes you can't help it. You can keep from swearing, though, or striking out to hurt someone."

Mama never criticized Grandpa for saying Darn or Dad-blast it, but she told us they were only substitutes for swear words. Sometimes I wondered what it would be like to come right out and holler, "Dammit to hell!"

At noon Mr. Simpson said, "You want to come in?" I said yes, for my mittens were soaked and my feet freezing. He let me put Chub in one of the empty stalls.

When we entered the kitchen his wife Maybelle was at the stove, the table set for two. Mr. Simpson swung a chair next to the open oven door. "You can put your things on that," he said. I hung my jacket over the chair back to face the oven and put my wet mittens on top. I pulled off my boots and stood them beside the stove.

"Here, take another chair," Mrs. Simpson offered. "Sit up to the oven and put your feet in." I settled down to eat.

Mr. Simpson sat at the table. "Where's my coffee?" he grunted.

"Keeping hot," said his wife and she took it from the stove. She looked at me. "Want a cup?"

"No thank you. I don't drink coffee."

She poured me a glass of cold milk. It helped wash down the icy peanut-butter sandwich.

"Eric fill the woodbox like I told him?" Mr. Simpson asked his wife.

"Yes, and he done his other chores. Jake, his hands're sticking through his mittens and he needs a new pair of galoshes. Snow's way over the tops."

"Have to wait'll I get this timber out, and the mill pays me."

"But he'll catch his death—"

"Can't help it, dammit. I'm down to my last dime."

Mama would say a man who can afford tobacco can clothe his family, I thought. Steam rose from my socks and the wool smelled singed. I chewed the last crust and drained my glass. Mr. Simpson inserted his chew of tobacco and rose from the table. We went out to face the storm.

Four hours later I hitched Chub to the ski-sled and drove home.

When the weekend came I waited for Mr. Simpson to mention money, but he didn't. On Monday morning at seven I was back at Simpsons. I saw Eric again carry a pail of milk, which slopped over as he staggered through the narrow path to the house. His red hands stuck out of his mittens and his galoshes let in snow. My mittens and long warm socks made me sorry for a little boy whose mother didn't knit.

I told Mama about Eric's mittens. She was all sympathy. "Poor boy. I'll knit him a pair. You get his size. Be sure to ask his mother." I didn't want to. I resented Mama's doing things for others when we didn't have enough ourselves. I knew it was part of her campaign to buy her way into Heaven. "If ye've done it unto the least of these, ye've done it unto Me."

As soon as Mama offered to knit Eric mittens I stopped feeling sorry for him. I asked Mrs. Simpson his hand size, though, and for three evenings had to watch Mama knit as she hummed, "Full of Beauty Is the Path of Duty." I delivered them to Eric on Friday in time for him to wear to school. He gave a bashful smile and mumbled, "Thank you." His mother sent her thanks to Mama.

Again, because it was week's end, I expected Mr. Simpson to hand me my pay. I had it figured: $13.50 for the first three days and a full week of nine-hour days, $22.50—a grand total of $36. He didn't say a word. "See you Monday," he called as I drove off. My mind was sore. I couldn't beg for my pay. I was mad at Mr. Simpson, but madder at myself. Why couldn't I speak up?

Mama was undisturbed. "He has to sell the logs first," she said. "When they pay him he'll pay you."

In January I was still working, piling up credit. "It's like money in the bank," I told Mama when I had to ask her for money to buy feed.

One Monday when I went to work I found the logs I had skidded all gone. "Mill hauled 'em over the weekend," said Mr. Simpson.

"When do you get paid?" I asked.

"Oh, I don't know."

"This month?" I persisted.

"Can't be sure." He reached in his pocket, drew out a plug and cut himself a fresh wad. "Afraid you won't get paid?" he asked.

"No. But I need money now for feed."

"Well, I'm sorry. I'm sure your mother'll help you. You see, my cows've got to eat too, and my wife and boy. I'll be hurting till the mill pays me."

The following Monday a cold sleet fell as I drove to work. When I went into the barn I found a horse standing in one of the stalls. Bales of hay were stacked in the corner and a black gelding munched at a brimful manger. Mr. Simpson finished the last cow and stood up. "How do you like him?" he asked with pride.

"He's all right," I said.

"Needs fattening," said Mr. Simpson, "but all that hay come with him." His voice was unnaturally hearty and he chewed and spit with vigor. "By the way, I won't need you after today. I'll skid my own logs now."

"That's all right," I said. The mill must have paid him, I thought. Now he'll pay me.

At quitting time Mr. Simpson said, "Thanks for helping out. Don't worry, you'll get your money."

"Not now?" I asked, bewildered.

"I'm a little short. Mill paid me, but the money didn't go round."

"You bought yourself a horse!"

"Yeah, it was the chance of a lifetime. Took all my cash. But I'll pay you, don't worry. Next batch of logs."

Blind with anger, I drove away. I told Mama what had happened.

"The very idea!" she said. "I'm going up there tomorrow and see that man. He can't do you like that, after all your work. You're going with me. After supper get a paper and set down what he owes you, like a bill."

We drove up at noon so Mr. Simpson would be in to dinner. Maybelle Simpson invited us in and cleared off a couple of chairs. The oven door was open, socks drying around it. I saw Mama's nose twitch at the smell and her eyes take in cobwebs in corners and a mess of litter swept under the table.

Mrs. Simpson offered us coffee but Mama declined. "I want to thank you for those mittens you knit my boy," said Mrs. Simpson. "He's wore 'em for weeks and they're just like new. Mighty warm, too."

"Just some scraps," Mama said. "Took me no time to knit."

Mr. Simpson came in. He stamped snow off and hung up his hat. He knew at once why Mama was there. "Howdy, ma'am. Glad to see you." He sat down at the table. "What's on your mind?"

"This is," she said smartly. She handed him the bill. It totaled $112.00.

"Yeah, that's what I owe her. She did a good job, too. I'll pay with my next batch of logs."

"We need the money now," she said. "She's got horses

to feed and I got a mortgage payment coming due."

Mrs. Simpson drooped. Her fork tumbled her food. She knew—we all knew—that he didn't intend to pay. "I ain't got the money," he said flatly. "There's just one thing I can do. My boy Eric's got a jigsaw his uncle gave him. If your daughter wants to settle for that I'd swap even. That saw's worth a hundred dollars."

"But it belongs to your boy," said Mama.

"No matter. He don't never use it."

"It's his'n, Jake," said his wife. "You oughtn't trade it off."

"No, we couldn't take it from the boy," said Mama. "We'll wait till you get the money."

I had always wanted a jigsaw, ever since Rajamak made the wooden horse. "Let's see it," I said to Mr. Simpson.

He rummaged in the other room and brought it out. It was an expensive model with a table that tilted, a guard around the blade, a pulley take-off for power. We didn't have power, but I thought Laurance could fix it to run by foot-power with our old treadle sewing machine. I could saw out figures, shape them with a knife and sell them. Before Mama could speak I said, "I'll take it."

"It's a deal," he said cordially and shook my hand.

"But, Jake—" Mrs. Simpson started, but her husband interrupted.

"Don't but me, woman. The boy don't never use it. It's just lying around."

"It was a present from Cy," she said.

"No matter. Here's a chance to get some use out of it."

When she could get a word in Mama said, "We wouldn't think of taking that saw away from your boy. Why, it belongs to him."

I turned to Mama. "What about *me*?" I cried. "The

money belongs to me. I earned it."

"But you wouldn't take it from a little boy!"

"That's between him and his father. I did the work. The saw's mine now."

I took the saw and went out to the car. Mama came. We rolled home in silence. At home I put the saw on my dresser to gloat over until Laurance would come home and fix it. When Eric's face began to haunt me I hid it in my closet. It still bothered me, so I took it to the attic and stuffed it behind some junk. When Laurance came home I brought the saw out and told him about my idea of foot power.

"Could be done," he said as he studied the saw. "Where'd you get this saw?"

I told him.

"You mean you stole that boy's saw?"

"His father owed it to me."

"That wasn't the boy's fault."

"I know," I said miserably. "But I wanted it. Otherwise I wouldn't get paid."

"That was a hateful thing to do," he said. "If I was you, I'd give it back."

"I can't. It's mine now."

"It's not yours, and never will be," said my brother. "And I'll have nothing to do with it." He left me and leaped down the stairs.

After that the saw hung like an albatross around my neck. Eric's face haunted my dreams. But I couldn't give it back. One day I took it out again. Water had leaked from the roof. The spurious chrome had tarnished. The blade was rusted and the table stuck fast. It was a relief to throw it away.

Hoofmarks

Laurance had come home for only a brief visit. He had a full-time summer job on the school farm and the next year would be his last. "It'll be my turn then," I said.

Mama said, "We'll see."

Again I raised crops and picked berries. I got a few jobs with my team, but Mabe could hardly work anymore, her heaves were so bad. She was almost thirty years old.

October came and we still didn't have winter hay. I sat on the partition between Mabe and Chub, watching Mabe try to eat. Her mule ears waggled as she mouthed the hay, spitting out most of it. Her ribs stuck out and her hip bones had begun to show. She coughed and cast up a cud of hay.

I left the stable, closing the door against a raw wind. Shriveled leaves reeled across the pasture, which was bitten down to the quick. I came into the kitchen where Mama was mixing bread. "Mabe needs more oats," I said. "She can't eat that hay."

Mama wiped flour from the sides of the bowl. "I can't spare the money," she said firmly. "I'm behind on the mortgage again and I must save a little for Laurance." Her hands pummeled the dough, which had become stubbornly resilient.

"But we can't let her starve!"

"You'd better put her out of the way," said Mama. "It would be the kindest thing to do."

"I can't."

"Well, what else? She's getting to be skin and bones and we just can't afford to feed her. You say her cough is worse. It's a shame to let her suffer." Her fists thudded against the dough while the wind whined around the chimney. "Have you got hay for winter?"

"Not enough. But I'll work with Chub."

"If he works he'll need more grain. I just can't manage. Rex Adams buys old horses for meat to feed his chickens. Think it over." She covered the bread and carried it to the stove. Lifting the lid she put in another stick of wood, her face flushed from the flames, a look of anguish in her eyes.

I rose from my chair and returned to the barn. Mabe's worn-out teeth still sorted the tough stems. She struggled to catch her breath. I went in beside her and stroked her lean neck and coarse mane, while I muttered meaningless words. Back in the kitchen I told Mama, "Tell Rex he can have her," and stalked to my room.

Next day Mama came home to say, "It's all settled. You take her over tomorrow and Rex'll shoot her. She won't suffer. He'll give you five dollars for her and you can buy feed for Chub."

Mabe followed behind the buggy as I drove Chub to Rex's place. We passed the pond where waterlilies grew thick and the man had scolded me once for picking an armful. We climbed the steep hill from which a view of the valley spread out with peaceful clusters of farm buildings and cows feeding in lush fall pasture. On a narrow side road we traversed the last mile to the Adams' yard.

Rex looked out from the door of the chicken house. "Tie her under the maple," he said. "I'll be right out."

I tied Mabe and drove around the house to leave Chub on the other side. Rex walked toward me. "I'll take care of her. Go on in the house." His mother came to the door and welcomed me in as Rex came back out with a gun over his arm. The door closed behind him. "Come on in the kitchen," said Mrs. Adams. "I'm churning and you can run the dash for me while I make up this cheese."

I heard the shot, followed by silence. Rex strode in. He leaned his gun against the door jamb and handed me Mabe's halter, still warm from her face, a few dark hairs caught in the buckle. From his thick billfold he gave me a five-dollar bill. I stumbled out the door and drove home.

A few days later I got a good skid job in Mr. Green's woodlot. Chub earned more than his keep and I made plans for school. Mama said I could begin at the second semester. She was going to work in the city again and there'd be nobody on the farm.

"What'll I do with Chub?" I asked as the time drew near.

"There's a Mr. Leon four miles up Taylor Road. I heard he needs a horse to haul timber this winter. Why not let him have Chub?—temporarily. Next summer you can bring him back here and find him a home."

I went to see Mr. Leon. He showed me a big barn with plenty of hay, and a comfortable stall. Something about him reminded me of Jake Simpson, but I let it go. Before I left for school I handed Chub over to work for his keep. He was fat and sassy as ever. I knew he'd do a good job.

I got back home for Easter. Mama wasn't there, but I wanted to see Chub. It was a cold, damp day as I hurried up to Leon's place. When I neared the farmhouse I saw a rough-coated nag in the barnlot, tugging forlornly at the frozen grass. His ribs were like a washboard and you could hang a hat on his hips. A wave of pity washed through me. I'd always hated to see a starved horse. Then I did a double-take. The horse was the color of Chub—as burlap can be the same shade as silk. I ran to the fence and called, "Chub!"

The horse lifted his head and the crooked blaze shone out. I vaulted the fence and ran to him, saying, "Chub! Chub! What have they done to you!" Taking his gaunt head in both hands I covered his nose with kisses. I looked into his dull eyes, fingered the unkempt mane. It was Chub.

The house door opened and Mr. Leon came toward me, his boots splashing through mud. He looked mad. Before he got close he was talking. "There's your horse, miss," he said. "And you can have him. I've never seen such a cantankerous, mean, balky critter in all my days. Get him off my place and good riddance. I fed him for you, but I couldn't get a lick of work out of him."

"Why didn't you tell my mother?" I asked, my voice shaking with rage.

"Your ma was away working. He's not so fat as he was,

but I can't stuff feed into an animal that won't work. I promised to keep him for you, anyway, and there he is. I'll go get your bridle."

I led Chub home. I couldn't bear to ride him. I wished I could carry him in my arms. There was no one at home to keep him, but I remembered Uncle Lewis. He still farmed with horses and though he was poor I knew he was kind. He and Chub would get along.

Uncle Lewis paid me forty dollars, and promised never to sell him. Next time I saw Chub he had filled out fine and he stepped with his old fire. Uncle Lewis joked about various maneuvers on Chub's part that had cost a smashed wheel or a broken trace chain. "He's a little dickens," he said fondly.

Whenever I visited Uncle Lewis I went into Chub's stall and spoke roughly to him so he wouldn't kick out, and as I stood beside his head I scolded him sternly so he wouldn't bite. Meanwhile I carefully studied his reactions, smoothing the flaxen mane and rubbing my hand over the silver hairs among the gold of his coat. He was restive as always under my caress, but I could tell he hadn't been abused.

Uncle Lewis came in the barn. "I like that little horse. He's got spunk." That was it, all right—what made me love him. Only I'd always called it spirit. He had the courage to keep going when he was scared; to pull his heart out, yet rebel against a tight rein; to be a willful eccentric, yet stick to the one principle he had learned in youth: "Whoa!"

"That's got me into more trouble!" declared Uncle Lewis. "How many times I've almost pitched over the dashboard when I've yelled 'No,' or 'Joe,' or anything that sounds like 'Whoa.'"

"I know what you mean!"

We laughed heartily together while Chub looked around and moved uneasily in his stall.

I knew that Chub would have to die sometime, but on that farm he would die among friends. At school I was busy with work and study. In my art classes I drew bluebirds in springtime, moonlit nights in the forest, and a horse like Chub standing in snow, wind blowing his mane. I was editor of the school paper and my writings were about life on the farm.

Every chance I got I went to see Chub and he was always the same. One Christmas I breezed in and asked Uncle Lewis, "How's Chub?"

"He's gone."

I was glad I hadn't been there to see him after his spirit left. It would have recalled the bitter day when I found him at Leon's with the light gone out of his eyes. It had been hard to forgive myself for that.

I said goodbye to Uncle Lewis and got in the Willys, which Mama had lent me for the trip. Before I turned the key I looked toward the stable where I'd seen Chub for the last time. They were all gone now—Tom with his white star; Mabe and her patient face; Chub on dancing feet. Gone forever, but in their going they had left hoofmarks in my heart that would never be erased. I turned the key of the old Willys and drove home to Tamarack Farm, where Mama was packing ready to take me back to school.